WARREN
BUFFETT

ACCOUNTING
BOOK

Reading Financial Statements
for Value Investing

Stig Brodersen and Preston Pysh

Library of Congress Cataloging-in-Publication Data

Brodersen, Stig
Pysh, Preston G.
    Warren Buffett Accounting Book
    p. cm.
    ISBN 978-1-939370-15-0
    1. Business & Investing. 2. Personal Finance. 3. Finance. 4. Investing.

Book Design by Pylon Publishing

This publication is designed to provide accurate and authoritative information in regards to the subject matter covered. It is sold with the understanding that neither the author nor the publisher is engaged in rendering legal, investment, accounting, or other professional services. If legal advice or other expert assistance is required, the services of a competent professional person should be sought.

ATTENTION: SCHOOLS AND BUSINESSES

Pylon Publishing books are available at quantity discounts with bulk purchase for educational, business, or sales promotional use. For information, please write to:

info@pylonpublishing.com

CONTENTS

CONTENTS

Preface

How to use this book

This book is the result of an evolving idea: everyday investors should not need a master's in finance to understand the fundamentals of Warren Buffett's investing approach. In 2012, we wrote a book titled *Warren Buffett's Three Favorite Books*. The book was written for amateur investors so they could understand the very basic and fundamental ideas around Warren Buffett's investing approach.

This book, however, takes investing to the next step—it teaches essential accounting terminology and techniques that serious stock investors need to know. The first four chapters of this book teach you how to think about the stock market, how to select and value stocks. Only limited accounting skills or knowledge will be required for this. If you want to dig further into corporate accounting, the last four chapters are where you will have a chance to get your hands dirty. This is where we will discuss the individual lines of accounting found on the three financial statements. Since this book's principles are based on the ideas of a few brilliant people, let's start with a brief introduction:

Warren Buffett (1930 -)

Starting out from nothing, Warren Buffett is now perceived as the greatest stock market investor of all time. His current net worth is in excess of $60 billion. His fortune has been built on a sound and consistent investment approach—which we will outline throughout this book. He is the CEO of a company called Berkshire Hathaway. Berkshire is an American conglomerate holding company, of which he is the largest shareholder. More than 99% of his net worth has been pledged to philanthropy.

PREFACE

Benjamin Graham (1894-1976)

By many, Graham is considered the founder of value investing. Benjamin Graham was Warren Buffett's professor at Columbia University, and was also Buffett's employer, mentor, and lifelong friend. Benjamin Graham is the author of the *The Intelligent Investor* and *Security Analysis*, undoubtedly the most important value investing literature ever written. Warren Buffett has, on several occasions, credited these books as shaping his philosophy as an investor.

Charles Munger (1924 -)

Vice-Chairman at Berkshire Hathaway and mainly known for being a business partner with Warren Buffett. Less known than Buffett, Charlie Munger is equally respected by value investors for his strong character and sound investment approach. Munger's investment talent has also made him a billionaire.

Chapter 1

How to Look at the Stock Market

Value investors view the stock market differently than other investors. They don't *believe* that the stock market consists of stocks. They *know* that the stock market consists of real companies. That little difference changes everything. It also explains why value investors consistently beat the stock market year after year.

In this chapter, you will learn how to think differently about the stock market. By thinking differently, you will have a distinct and unique advantage that will lead to growth, reduce risk, and create less stress. You will learn why it is good when stock prices drop, and why the wise stock investor will grow wealthy over time.

Mr. Market and bubbles in the market

Have you met Mr. Market? If you have ever traded on the stock exchange, you have met him. If you have listened to financial news, you have heard about him for sure. Mr. Market is a fictitious person about whom the founder of value investing, Professor Benjamin Graham, taught to his class at Columbia University in the 1950s. Perhaps you have heard of Graham? If not, I'm sure you will have heard of one of his brilliant students: his name is Warren Buffett and he is the most successful stock investor in history.

Mr. Market is a very important person to familiarize yourself with if you are serious about stock investing. Every day he comes by to visit you.

When he arrives, you can buy or sell high- and/or low-quality companies. It is always nice to get a visit from Mr. Market. He doesn't get offended easily. You can look at his companies as much as you want—every day if you wish—and you don't have to buy or sell anything. You can wait as long as you would like. The best part about Mr. Market is that you can ignore him for years, yet he will keep coming back every day with new offers.

Sometimes when Mr. Market arrives, he is in a good mood. When this happens, Mr. Market has a lot of customers and the prices are high for all of his products—both the high-quality and low-quality companies. The next day when Mr. Market visits, there might be very few customers. As one might expect, Mr. Market will not be in a good mood. On these days, the companies Mr. Market is selling are on sale; therefore, the price for the exact same company is cheaper.

Yes, you probably have guessed what we are talking about. We are talking about the stock market. The stock market moves up and down every day. Some may argue that there is always a reason for stock price fluctuations. They think the current price always reflects the true value of the company. This idea is especially popular within academia.

Value investors like Warren Buffett and Benjamin Graham strongly disagree. They believe the stock market moves in the short term due to emotions and in the long term due to value. Mr. Market may be a fictitious character, but he's a symbol of the emotional psychology the stock market follows in the short term. There is good reason to believe that Warren Buffett is right: he's accumulated over 60 billion dollars in personal wealth using value investing.

For many investors, the stock market remains a puzzle. They see a lot of different prices that move up and down. They base their actions on hope with the expectation that they can buy cheap and sell high. Now, you'll notice I referred to them as *investors*. I would like to withdraw that. In my humble opinion, these people are *traders*. The world has always had a lot of traders. Five hundred years ago, Europeans sailed to the new world to buy tobacco and sell it for a higher price back home. When you are shopping for groceries, you are buying milk at a higher price than the store bought it for. Trading is a technique. It does not matter whether it is tobacco, milk or stocks.

If you are a value investor, you don't see a stock. You see a company. Many people tend to forget that, when owning a stock, you really own an equally divisible share of a real business. This means the ownership of one share is the same exact thing as owning every share—the value is completely proportional. The stock market gives each investor a unique opportunity to invest in real companies—as an owner—and proportionally share the company's profits. Now, Warren Buffett may own a bigger part of Coca-Cola than you can afford, but the principle is exactly the same. If you want to be a value investor like Warren Buffett, you want to accumulate stocks, not trade them. Benjamin Graham has a quote: "In the short run, the market is a voting machine, but in the long run it is a weighing machine." This profound statement signifies his ideology that accumulating more shares—or equity—in the business is paramount over the day-to-day activity of the market.

Another important thing to understand about the stock market is that there is often a reason stock prices are moving. That said, changes in stock prices don't necessarily mean that they are *logical* or *fundamental*. You often see stock XYZ increase 2% from one day to the next—then drop 1% the day after. That does not seem to puzzle most people. But if you think about it, the argument you hear often makes no sense. Assume Company XYZ is Coca-Cola. You hear an analyst on TV who says that the increase in the stock price is because the latest job report was better than expected. Then, within 24 hours, you hear another analyst suggest that the same stock decreased in value because consumer confidence is lower than the big investment banks expected. Does that really explain why Coca-Cola is more valuable on one day than another? Clearly the answer is no. If we were conducting day-to-day valuations of a small business on the streets of small town U.S.A, it's quite humorous to think of such a scenario.

Who determines the stock price? Everyone participating in buying and selling stocks is influencing the constantly changing stock prices. Typically, less than 1% of total ownership is traded during a day. Those few traders are ultimately determining the current price through the supply and demand of the shares. Very often, it is these same people who are *trading*. The price of a company is therefore being determined by hundreds if not thousands of factors each and every day. Some traders have analytical justification for their trading; many others have emotional or personal reasons. Again, please meet Mr. Market!

Please note that I am talking about the *price*; I am not talking about the *value* of the stocks—not yet at least. Price and value are completely different things. When Mr. Market is in high spirits and prices are high, we sometimes experience a bubble. It occurs when there is no sustainable relationship between the value and the price of a company.

We have seen a bubble burst in the stock market many times before. One example is the dot-com bubble in 2000 which was driven by an overly optimistic faith in technology companies. The belief was that any price was justifiable to own such a business. Like any other bubble, this idea was dangerously wrong. Recently, the world experienced a real-estate bubble which littered banks with bad loans. Once again, this bubble popped and the situation corrected once price and value had no sustainable relationship to each other.

Why do these bubbles keep occurring? Have we learnt nothing from history? The most obvious answer must be no. In 1637, we had the first recording of an economic bubble. It was in the Netherlands when "Tulipmania" occurred. At the peak of the bubble, a tulip bulb was traded at the price of 10 years' annual income for a worker, far greater than the *value* of a tulip bulb. Today we might have a laugh at the expense of the poor Dutch people who went into economic ruin, but as we have seen twice in the last decade, humanity has learned very little from historic economic bubbles.

We have experienced economic bubbles on a regular basis for a very long time, and there's strong reasoning to suggest more are on the way.

The argument is simple: bubbles are created by people, and while it is possible to predict that most people will do something unwise in the stock market, it is impossible to predict for how long. We may know that there is a bubble, but we don't know when it will burst. It may take years. Many people have lost a lot of money betting against the market in a bubble, and even if they were right, they often run out of money before the market makes a correction.

Betting *against* human behavior is speculating. But let's take a look at why value investing is about benefiting from human behavior. We will teach you what Benjamin Graham taught his students:

> *"Mr. Market is your servant, not your guide."*—Warren Buffett

Good news! The market is dropping

Do you like to shop for deals? I sure do! Who doesn't like to buy a quality product at a cheaper price? I buy more stuff when prices are low. Then, when the price increases, I buy less, or none.

It's funny; when people buy items at the store, this is likely how they shop—yet, interestingly, when it comes to buying stocks, they do the exact opposite. Why?

Chapter 1 How to Look at the Stock Market

When stock markets are trading at high levels, you'll often find people are flocking towards the idea of easy money. In contrast, when the market is down or performing poorly, common traders avoid the market like the plague. This likely happens because individuals substitute group thinking for true understanding and knowledge; therefore, when the market is performing poorly, these individuals leave because they inherently acknowledge that they are dealing with a situation they don't understand. This idea is important. At the root of value investing is this fundamental idea: The market doesn't offer value; it offers price. You must determine value and you must always remember that it is seldom a poor decision to buy something for $5.00 when it's actually worth $10.00.

As a stock investor, you should almost always hope for the market to drop. There is one rare exception: when you're bound by time. If you are looking to retire within a year or two, for example, and need access to a large portion of your savings, the stock market is probably a risky place to have your money. If time isn't a concern, you should hope that stocks are as cheap as possible.

Remember Mr. Market? Previously we saw that when he was in a good mood, prices were very high; conversely, when he was in a bad mood, prices were low. In martial arts, there's a term called Aikido. This means you use your opponent's momentum against him. As a value investor, you might not feel comfortable referring to the other person as your opponent, but there is definitely symbolic importance to using the other person's momentum. When Mr. Market is in a bad mood, it is the time to accumulate stock and start *using* the inevitable human behavior to your advantage. Remember, poorly performing stock markets are your advantage—if you choose and act on them wisely.

You know that the market price is determined in the short run by human psychology. At some point in time, people will be fearful and stocks will be very cheap. In contrast, other times will present greedy periods where prices are high. We can't predict the future, but we can reasonably assume fear and greed will continue to play an active role in market movements in the future.

Stock prices jump up and down like crazy. As a value investor, you should not let this discourage you in any way. In fact, this should excite you. Mr. Market is your servant, and the more severe his mood swings, the better deals you're afforded. His violent swings in price will only allow you to buy cheaper and sell higher.

One important skill that separates the great investors from the majority of mediocre investors is that great investors can control their emotions. Great investors like Warren Buffett are not discouraged when the stock price of one of their investments drops. When Warren Buffett has determined that he is indeed paying $5.00 for something that's worth $10.00, it is great news if the price drops to $4.00. At $4.00, he can buy even more shares than he could earlier.

For most people, this idea is counterintuitive. If they buy something, they hope that item will increase in price shortly after their purchase. The problem for these types of investors is their minds are bound by time. In order for value investing to work, you must remove the time element that often dictates impulsive decisions. The best way to remove this impulse is to increase your level of knowledge. As your knowledge increases, your confidence improves and your understanding of truth and facts becomes clear. Financial education removes the time and impulse element found in novice investors. As you progress throughout this book, I'm confident you'll start to develop a sincere excitement for bear markets—or slang for markets moving lower.

Why stocks will make you wealthy

Stocks are a simple—but not easy—way of getting wealthy. The simplicity of a stock can be shown by realizing that when you own a stock you own a tiny piece of a real business. Think of one share as its own entity or mini business. If you want to imagine it as being small enough to fit in the palm of your hand, go ahead. It might actually make more sense that way. Staying with this visual example, now imagine that this palm-sized business makes a small product; it has small employees and a small inventory. You can take this example as far as you would like, but the point is this: one share produces the exact same profit or loss as the entire business. This visualization will really help later on when you think of owning 100 tiny businesses that each produce a $1 profit and they each cost $10 to own.

This also means that as long as companies make a profit over time, the owners of those companies will eventually accumulate wealth. So, if stocks are as simple as I have just described, why don't more people get wealthy through the stock market?

Well, most people would rather rely on the promise of getting rich tomorrow than the certainty of getting rich in twenty to thirty years. This opinion can be substantiated by the fact that more people play the lottery than invest in the stock market. Remember, special skills are not required to become wealthy in the stock market.

So as you look at the world of investing with an open perspective, you're probably wondering if stocks are the most lucrative path forward. If that is your line of thought, you should be proud. Of the variety of investment possibilities in this world, only a few categories generate income on a consistent basis. Stocks, as a whole, are one of them.

The distinction between investments that generate profit and those that do not is important to consider. A category that does not generate income is precious metal. Examples could be gold, silver or diamonds: while a company generates wealth back to the owner from profit, a piece of gold does not produce anything. There is no cash flow generated back to you. The only way you can make money in gold is if someone thinks that the piece of gold is worth more than you paid for it. History has also shown that there is something to it. From 1900-2000, the Dow Jones went from 66 to 11497, while gold went from $20 to $400.

Before you even start to think about entering a new investment, always ask: "Does it generate any cash flow back to me?" You will soon realize that investments like precious metals, wine and art are bad alternatives to stocks because they don't create consistent cash flow.

Now, I have been very general in this discussion so far. I have established why the stock market is suitable for compounding your wealth; however, as a real investor, you're probably not satisfied with a generic assessment that "Stocks have always gone up because they are businesses." An investor also wants to maximize his return within this investment category of stocks. In order to accomplish that mission, you need to be armed with a few economic concepts and some simple accounting. This book's goal is to provide those tools for you.

Chapter 2
Concepts Every Investor Should Know

If you really want to beat the stock market, you should start studying stocks—right? Learn all about P/E, ROE, profit ratio and so on? Well, not yet.

No investor has ever beaten the stock market on a consistent basis without understanding interest rates, inflation and bonds. Now, this might sound like a dry topic, but your success in the stock market is intimately tied to your firm understanding of this chapter. A lot of people try, and many fail. But that is not you. You have decided to go the extra mile and study these concepts. And guess what? There are seldom traffic jams on the extra mile.

Interest rates

You hear about it in the news all the time: the interest rate. The interest rate never seems to relax, and it's always going up or down. But what is the interest rate *really*, and why is it important for you, as a stock investor?

Think of interest rates like gravity. Gravity has a persistent impact on the way you live your life; for example, whether you go to bed or you run a marathon, you're experiencing gravity. Like gravity, the interest rate has a persistent impact on money and businesses. It is always there.

Unlike gravity, interest rates fluctuate. They are persistent, or always there, but they are also changing in magnitude. To visualize this from a practical standpoint, let's return to our analogy.

"A Rare Glimpse of the Interest Rate".

Let's assume you live on a planet where gravity changes once a day. The first day, gravity is normal. We will baseline this gravity at 1.0. On this particular day, you go about your normal business and don't have any issues. As we move to the next day, something interesting happens: gravity goes higher. It moves to 2.0. This means that everything is twice as heavy and difficult to lift and move. On the second day, you find yourself less willing to run and work because it takes twice the amount of work to do the same job as the previous day. Finally, as we move to the third day, gravity experiences a sharp change and it's now at 0.50. This is a very interesting change and dynamic for you to experience because everything is extremely light and easy to move. Your body and objects weigh ¼ that of the previous day. This extreme difference promotes your ability to run faster and perform more work. Needless to say, life becomes really easy.

As we look at this odd example, it has significant importance to your fundamental understanding of financial markets: interest rates work like gravity.

When interest rates rise, business becomes more difficult and vulnerable. This is because businesses can't borrow money at cheap and affordable prices. When interest rates decrease, business becomes easier and less vulnerable. The value of previously held assets increases because more and more people can borrow money, which increases demand, and their monthly payments are now lower if they need to borrow money to buy.

Businesses experience interest rates in this manner. When interest rates rise, only the strongest and fittest business can endure the change. Their profits are handicapped by their inability to move and remain agile.

Moving into the more technical description of interest rates, you can think of it as the *price of money*. Imagine that you have just found a beautiful new house and you are looking at two different funding options. One bank offers you a thirty-year mortgage of 6% and another bank offers a similar loan at 4%. If the seller wants $300,000 for the house, your total annual interest payment for the house would be $18,000 and $12,000 respectively. Don't think about the math for now; just realize that the lower interest rate makes the house more affordable to more people than the 6% rate. This increased affordability at 4% allows more buyers into the market for the $300,000 house, increasing demand and potentially the asking price ($300,000). As you can see, the price of the house remained fixed at $300,000, but the value did not. As we look at the possibility of the asking price increasing due to demand at the lower interest rate, this is a slow process that may take months or years. As you can see, the difference between interest rates creates a disparity between price and value. This disparity is where an investor makes money—especially in the stock market.

That sounds simple doesn't it? Well, interest rates *can* be very simple, and the basic principle is always the same: the borrower has to pay the interests to the lender, and the interest rate is specified when the agreement is made.

When you hear about interest rates in the news, it is most often the "government bond interest rate," which is determined by the United States Federal (FED) Reserve. The FED is an independent organization that manages the money supply and fiscal policy for the U.S. Government. Almost all modern countries have their own federal reserve. One of the most important jobs of the Federal Reserve is to influence interest rates for their citizens. Now, there's a huge debate about whether the Federal Reserve creates stability or instability for the economy by adjusting interest rates, but that's not important. As an investor, the important thing to understand is that the FED purposely adjusts the interest rates to improve and slow the growth of the economy. Without controlling this rate, many argue the financial system(s) may collapse due to enormous market bubbles or lack of credit/cash in the system. Every time interest rates change, so does the disparity between price and value—therefore creating potential opportunities.

As a stock investor, it is extremely important to keep an eye on the interest rate. You should act differently in the stock market when the interest is low compared to when it is high. Why? To answer this question, let's look at how interest rates are generally determined.

Imagine that you just found the TV of your dreams. It is 60 inches, smooth design and the picture is sharp as a razor. Unfortunately, it costs $1,000 and you don't have that kind of money for a TV. The store clerk then gives you an amazing offer: get the TV on credit! No down payment, and he will even arrange free delivery. Looking at the terms and conditions, you see that the interest rate is 20%; in other words, the price of money is very high. You will need to pay $200 every year for the rest of your life if you don't pay off the principal! The TV does not look so good now, does it?

We saw earlier that the interest rate of a mortgage was as low as 4%. Why is there such a difference in cost for borrowers? Is the bank just a friendlier lender than the store clerk in the electronic store? No, the reason is *risk*. With the house, the bank can simply repossess the house and recover a large portion of their loan if you default on the loan. With the TV, it's a different story. A used TV may only fetch half the value it was previously sold for. Within a few years, the TV may be worth a hundred dollars. Since the interest rate is the price of money, it is also how the lenders adjust to financial circumstances, which is then reflected in your financial behavior as a consumer.

The FED determines the interest rate in a similar way. They look at risk and how to adjust financial behavior; however, they do it on a much larger *macro* scale. The FED is not only looking at you, but at the whole economy. In times of recession, the government wants us to spend more money. It achieves this by lowering the price of money. In other words, it lowers interest rates. This is an incentive to spend more money. When more money is spent, it will increase consumption, which in turn will lead to employment and higher wealth in the economy. When interest rates are low, companies can borrow for less. This makes new investments more attractive, which again leads to more employment and higher wealth. When money is cheap, typically stocks are too. This is the most important time to accumulate as many shares as you can.

When times are good, the government wants it to continue. They achieve this by trying to avoid a bubble in the market—so they increase the price of money, or increase interest rates. When things get expensive, we tend to buy less. That is not only true for TVs and houses; we adjust our financial behavior to all consumption. As with the electronic store that is lending you money for a TV, the risk and thereby the interest rate is high. Citizens really do not want a bubble, and even less a bubble that bursts, because it creates instability in the economy. As a successful stock investor, bubbles and interest rate swings present enormous opportunities.

If you want to master the stock market, start with a firm understanding of interest rates. It's truly the foundation to the entire economic cycle and *value* of everything on the planet. Remember, there's a big difference between price and value, and interest rates are the key ingredient to their disparity. Determining this difference will be the ultimate key to your success.

Inflation

You want to become a millionaire? The good news is that it's easier for you than your grandparents.

You guessed it; I am talking about inflation. Every year, the prices of goods and services increase a little. We are only talking a few percentage points, but when you add it all up, $1 in 1913 would cost as much as $23.49 in 2013.

Why do we have inflation at all? Is inflation good? And why is this even remotely interesting for you as a stock investor?

First things first! Let's discuss why we have inflation. To start this discussion, we would like to ask you whether you would like to buy your groceries today for $100 or the exact same basket of goods tomorrow for $103? What would you do? Well, most likely you would choose to buy the goods today. I would do the same! Let's buy it cheap!

Inflation works in the same way, though not quite as fast. The government likes a little inflation for three reasons. The first reason is that you consume more, and as a result, your purchases start generating employment and wealth in society.

You might wait longer than one day, but the same basket of groceries that cost $100 today will at some point cost $103. The way the Federal Reserve does this is through increasing the number of dollars in the economic system. Simply put, they keep adding more and more dollars to the system so the prices slowly increase over time. An important notion you need to understand is the difference between nominal dollars and real dollars. Nominal dollars don't account for inflation. Real dollars do. So if Grandpa says he earned $1 an hour in 1913, he's actually saying that he earned $1 nominal dollar. If Grandpa was an economics major, he might say he earned $1 nominal dollar an hour in 1913, which is equivalent to $23.49 real dollars (or today dollars).

The second reason the government likes a little inflation is that you are being taxed on nominal dollars. Let's take an example: You just bought an asset for $100,000. Next year, the price of the asset is $102,000 due to inflation of 2%. There is no real appreciation on the value of the asset, but since you get taxed on the growth on the nominal value (the $2,000 gain), the inflation itself taxes you. You can also look at it like this: You can sell your asset a year after, but you will not be able to buy more for that money. Actually, you have a little less since you need to pay your taxes!

The third reason is that debt is issued in nominal terms. As you probably know, the U.S. Government has a lot of debt. That enormous amount of debt is easier to pay back as time marches on because the money supply gradually inflates. We will look in greater detail at the concept of *real dollars* versus *nominal dollars* in just a bit.

From a government standpoint, inflation seems good, doesn't it? It might be advantageous for a government, but not for the individual investor. From your vantage point, inflation is a constant drag or friction on your ability to make returns.

Too much inflation creates uncertainty, and that is not good for lenders, companies, consumers or the exchange rate. There will be fewer investments and spending, which, as we have just learned, is not good for employment and general wealth in society. Too much inflation also means that people living on fixed incomes, such as pension benefits, experience less buying power for their money as time goes on. This brings us back to the concept of *real dollars*. We are interested in what we can buy for our money—not how much money we have. Or if you are in debt, like our government, you are also interested in the *real* value of your debt. When talking about inflation and the difference between real and nominal dollars, one should really consider what money is.

What is money? Well, money is just what we agree it is in society. There has always been some sort of currency. Native Americans used wampum. The only reason dollars are of any value is because we know that you and everybody else in society have a common understanding and trust in the value of dollars.

We only value dollars with respect to what we can buy with them. That is the real value of the dollar. That is why it is so important, as a stock investor, that you understand inflation. To get a rough estimate, the math is pretty simple: if you make a 10% nominal return on your stocks one year and inflation is 2%, you have a real return of approximately 8%.

That actually adds up to a lot over time. If you invested $1 in a 10% stock in 1913, you would now have as much as $13,781 a century later; however, if you subtracted annualized inflation of 2%, you would only have $2,200 in real dollars in 2013!

Even though inflation diminishes your return, being a stock investor is not as bad as it sounds. For one thing, you can't do anything about inflation; it diminishes your return no matter what you invest in. In general, debts (or bonds) are completely impacted by inflation, and stocks are partially impacted by inflation. As we advance through the book, you'll understand why.

Bonds

What is sexy and can get you rich in less than a year? I would certainly like to know the answer if you have one! I am certain the answer is not bonds. That said, I am certain that your understanding of bonds is equally as important as your understanding of stocks and interest rates.

What does history tell us about the return for bonds compared to stocks?

From 1928-2011, long-term bonds averaged 5.4% and stocks averaged 11.2%. *So why get so excited about bonds?* you might ask. Doesn't this statistic tell us that we should put all of our money into stocks instead of bonds? Well, from 2002-2011, long-term bonds averaged yearly returns of 6.85% and stocks 4.93%, so the picture is not so clear. What this shows us is that sometimes bonds are the preferred choice—and sometimes stocks are.

So, let's dig into it and see what bonds are really about. A bond is a loan. Yes, it is that simple! A bond is just an agreement that you are lending someone else money. It could be a company or the government. I personally like the idea of the government owing us money for a change!

In any case, the borrower has an obligation to pay back your loan. A bond consists of three simple components:

1) Par value or face value. This is the amount that the bond is issued for. Also, the par value is the amount you get back when the bond matures.
2) Term. This is the duration of the bond until it matures.
3) Coupon or Interest rate. The amount of money that you get back every year as a percentage of the par value.

Let's take a simple example to show how bonds work:

Par value	$1,000
Term	30 years
Coupon rate	5%

So, in this situation, you will lend out $1,000 to own the bond. The term of the ownership (or loan) is 30 years. For your courtesy, you will receive $50 each year until it matures 30 years later. Also, at the end of those 30 years, you'll get the par value of $1,000 back. In total you will receive $2,500 (30 years x $50 + $1,000). This equates to a $1,500 profit in nominal dollars.

Now, this is where it gets very interesting. We have just learned about interest rates and inflation and why these are important for you as a stock investor.

We have also learned that the interest rate was the *price of money*. So when the interest rate is high, the price of money is also high. That means that if you're the lender (or bond purchaser), you will receive more money from the borrower (or bond seller) if interest rates across the market are generally high.

Now, we are not only talking about the government interest rate. Companies can also issue bonds and have their own interest rates. As one might expect, an unhealthy company will issue bonds at a higher interest rate than healthy ones. In fact, company rates are often higher than those of the government because companies are more likely to fail.

Does this mean you should be investing in bonds rather than stock when interest rates are high? Perhaps! To answer that question, we also need to consider inflation and expected yields of all opportunities.

Going back to the previous example where we had a $1,000 bond with a 5% coupon (or $50 a year), let's look at how a 5% inflation rate would impact this investment. Throughout the duration of that thirty-year bond, the government would be inflating the value of the currency so rapidly that your 5% coupon growth would be completely offset by the 5% inflation. As a result, your real return would be nothing. Now, you would still receive your par value of $1,000 back at the end of the 30 years, and you would still receive $1,500 in coupon payments over the 30-year period, but your purchasing power will remain unchanged.

Takeaways from this chapter

Let me summarize the interaction between interest rates, inflation, bonds and stocks here:

	Low interest rates	High interest rates
Low inflation	Stocks	Bonds
High inflation	Stocks	Stocks

Bonds are preferred in the situation where inflation is low and interest rates are high. That is partly because inflation diminishes the fixed income received from bonds, but also because a high-interest environment may yield better returns. In all other cases, stocks are likely the preferred choice. As the book progresses, I'll provided more definitive guidance on which type of investment you should consider and why.

Chapter 3
A Brief Introduction to Financial Statements

For most people, financial reports are as interesting as looking at paint dry. Some might even say that paint is more interesting since we understand the function of paint. Financial reports, on the other hand... What is the purpose of them? Before I answer that relatively simple question, let's get one thing straight: Financial statements are not as complicated as you might think! You may need to think a little differently than you are used to, but with a little practice and guidance you will be amazed how simple they really are.

In the second half of the book, I will go in depth into each line of various financial statements and speak more about how the different statements are related. But before that, this chapter will give you a quick and easy overview of the content found in financial statements.

You can look at financial statements as systematic reports that inform you about the successes or failures of a company. At the end of the day, there's nothing more important to consider when you're looking to own a business—i.e., how does this company make a profit and what are they currently worth. If I wanted to make financial statements about you, I would write down on a piece of paper how much money you made and how much you spent. On another piece of paper, I might keep track of your long-term savings and debts—like the balance on your IRA account or mortgage. And perhaps on a third piece of paper, I might keep track of every transaction you've made from your cash and/or checking account.

These three pieces of paper would really give me a good idea about your current worth and what earnings capacity you potentially have.

That sounds simple—right? It is simple and it is really the essence of financial statements. When you collect these three pieces of paper in one major pool of information, you have a report about your personal finances. Companies do the same thing about their finances: they consolidate every piece of information into a big report, and refer to that as their quarterly or annual report.

In an annual report, you will see several important statements of varying relevance. The three most important reports are called the income statement, the balance sheet and the cash flow statement. When you start looking into value investing, these are really the main statements to focus on. Let's take a brief look at each of them.

The income statement

How much profit does a company make in one year? That is really the question that is being asked in the income statement. If you see an income statement for a company, it may look confusing with all the technical accounting terms.

Although this might seem intimidating, Chapter 6 explains each of the accounting terms in detail. For now, all you need to keep in mind is that the income statement is determining how much profit the company has made in one year (for an annual report). That is also why the income statement is often referred to as the profit and loss statement. It summarizes how much money the company has made during the year and how much it has spent. The difference is the profit (or the loss), which you can find at the very bottom. Profit, earnings—more commonly known as net income—are all terms for the same thing. It's important that you remember those three terms.

Income statement		in millions
1	Revenue	13,279
2	Cost of revenue	5,348
1-2 = 3	Gross Margin	7,931
4	Sales and Marketing expenses	1,105
5	Research and development expenses	863
6	General and Administration expenses	538
7	Other operating expenses	1,350
4+5+6+7 = 8	Operating expenses	3,856
3-8 = 9	Income from operations	4,075
10	Net interest income/(expenses)	(135)
11	Extraordinary income/(expenses)	275
12	Income taxes	1,352
9+10+11-12 = 13	Net income	2,863

Another way of looking at the income statement is to consider your personal finances. The principle is exactly the same. If I asked you how much money you made last year from your job, you may answer $20,000. That is your revenue. This would be the top line of the income statement for you.

Basically, all other transactions during a year except your paycheck are expenses. You typically have different types of expenses from your daily living. Everybody has expenses for either rent or mortgage. You need new clothes from time to time, and you obviously need to eat. There is also a variety of different expenses that you cannot avoid one way or the other, and here I have called them "other expenses." Below, I have prepared a simple income statement to illustrate what your personal income statement might look like.

Salary	$ 20,000
Housing expenses	$ -10,000
Clothing	$ -1,000
Food	$ -3,000
Other expenses	$ -2,500
Profit (Loss)	$ 3,500

As you can see, the resemblance between the income statement for your personal finances and that of a company is very similar. A company would label your annual salary *revenue*. As a private person, you may make your annual salary from working at a restaurant. The restaurant's income statement would label its sale of hamburgers as *revenue*.

While you will have expenses for housing, clothes and food, the restaurant will also have expenses, but may label these as *production costs* or *selling and administration costs*. As you already know, expenses are subtracted from the salary (individual) or revenue (company). The difference between the revenue and expenses is what the company calls *net income* or *net profit*. This is obviously a very important number.

In accounting and investing, income (or earnings) is often dividend into a per share basis which is called earnings per share (EPS). If the above example was showing earnings from a company with 100 shares, the EPS would be $3,500/100 = $35. If we were going to find the EPS of the real income statement initially displayed, we would take the net income of $2,863 and divided it by the number of shares outstanding. Assuming the shares outstanding are 100 (for simplicity), the EPS would be $28.63.

This is an extremely important number because it represents the profit of the company for each share.

Keep this very basic foundation at the forefront of your mind as I explain the income statement in detail during Chapter 6.

The balance sheet

"How much am I really worth"? That's an interesting question, isn't it? The main purpose of the balance sheet is to answer that question. If you look at a balance sheet for a company, it may look something like this:

	Assets	
1	Cash and cash equivalents	1,847
2	Accounts receivable	3,897
3	Inventory	2,486
4	Other current assets	638
5	Prepaid expenses	285
1+2+3+4+5 = 6	Total current assets	9,153
7	Non-current receivables	1,811
8	Non-current investments	2,768
9	Property, plant, and equipment	8,292
10	Patents, trademarks, and other intangibles	1,827
11	Goodwill	3,235
7+8+9+10+11 = 12	Total non-current assets	17,933
6+12 = 13	Total assets	27,086

	Liabilities	
1	Accounts payable	2,183
2	Notes payable	498
3	Accrued expenses	854
4	Taxes payable	427
1+2+3+4 = 5	Total current liabilities	3,962
6	Long term debt	3,211
7	Deferred tax	1,242
8	Provisions	273
6+7+8 = 9	Total non-current liabilities	4,726
5+9 = 10	Total liabilities	8,688
11	Share capital	400
12	Additional paid in capital	3,261
13	Retained earnings	15,590
14	Treasury stocks	-853
11+12+13+14 = 15	Total equity	18,398
10+15 = 16	Total liabilities and equity	27,086

I know. It may look very complicated, and there are a lot of new accounting terms that you might have never seen. But in essence, the company is just asking, "How much am I worth right now?"

Again, I think that we should return to your personal finances to see how simple a balance sheet really is. I want you to list all your personal belongings that you currently have. These are called *assets* because they are something you own. Okay, start writing everything down:

Car	$20,000
Home	$150,000
Furniture	$2,500
etc...	

Then you should consider how much debt you have attached to each of these assets. We call these *liabilities* because they are something that you owe to somebody else. This could be the car dealership, the bank, or any place you have incurred debt to finance your assets. Assuming you have your car and home partially financed, your balance sheet may look something like this:

Assets		Liabilities	
Car	$ 20,000	Car debt	$ 15,000
Home	$ 150,000	Mortgage	$ 120,000
Furniture	$ 3,000		
	$ 173,000		$ 135,000

So now we know the value of what you own, and how much you have borrowed to be able to buy these assets. We only need to complete one simple step before we are done: we need to make the balance sheet... balance. The total assets must equal the total liabilities—which is not the case at the moment. The idea behind this is very simple: the assets are what you own, and they are financed by two, and only two, options.

You can finance your assets with other people's money—for example, the bank. We call this a *liability*. Or you can finance them with your own money, and we call this *equity* or sometimes *shareholders' equity*. Equity is very easy to calculate as it is the difference between what you own (assets), and what you have borrowed (liabilities). In this example, we would calculate it like this: $173,000-$135,000 = $38,000

If we insert the difference, it looks like this:

Assets		Liabilities	
Car	$ 20,000	Equity	$ 38,000
Home	$ 150,000	Car debt	$ 15,000
Furniture	$ 3,000	Mortgage	$ 120,000
	$ 173,000		$ 173,000

Now the balance sheet is complete. And we have an answer to our original question: "How much am I really worth?" The answer in this generic example is $38,000.

Balance sheets for companies work the same way. Companies may own more cars and buildings, but the principles are exactly the same for their balance sheets.

I like to think about the balance sheet like this: An asset is what the company owns. These assets are either financed with their own money (equity) or by someone else's money; for example, the bank (liabilities).

Then you might ask, *Why is equity grouped with liabilities?* Since it is the company's money, should it not be under assets? The answer is very simple! Equity or shareholders' equity does not technically belong to the company; it simply belongs to the shareholders. In other words, the equity is a liability to the company because that is what the company owes to the shareholders.

In investing and accounting, equity is often referred to as book value. In order to determine the book value, you'll need to divide the equity into a per share basis. Looking at the balance sheet that was initially presented in this section, you can calculate its book value by finding the equity of $18,398 (found on line 15 of the liabilities column). Take that number and divide it by the number of shares outstanding. For demonstration purposes, let's assume the company has 100 shares outstanding. This means our book value (or equity per share) would be 18,398/100 = $183.98. This is a very important number to understand, so make sure you don't move forward until you understand this concept. At the bottom of every income statement and balance sheet, you'll find an area that states the number of shares outstanding.

If you understood everything in this short explanation, you're off to a great start. Feel free to return to this short section if you get confused by the details in Chapter 7 and beyond. This foundation is extremely important.

The cash flow statement

"Cash is King." Many people have heard this expression about finance and investing, and perhaps wondered why something so obvious has drawn so much attention. You seldom hear people say, "I like sunshine better than rain" or, "I would rather be full than hungry." Since we obviously would rather have cash than *not* have it, what does "Cash is King" mean?

To understand this simple expression, one needs to take a look at a company's cash flow statement. It may look something like this:

1	Net Income	2,863
2	Depreciation	516
3	Other non-cash items	264
4	Deferred taxes	287
5	Working capital	-832
1+2+3+4+5=6	Cash flow from operating activities	3,098
7	Property, plant, and equipment, net	-1,349
8	Intangible assets, net	-214
9	Businesses, net	86
10	Investments, net	-176
7+8+9+10 = 11	Cash flow from investing activities	-1,653
12	Issuances of common stock	98
13	Purchase of stock for treasury	-326
14	Payment of cash dividends	-682
15	Issuances/payment of debt (net)	-120
12+13+14+15 = 16	Cash flow from financing activities	-1,030
6+11+16 = 17	Change in cash	415
18	Cash and equivalents, start of period	1,432
17+18 = 19	Cash and equivalents, end of period	1,847

Again, on the surface, this looks complicated, but after a little practice, it becomes very simple. First, let's take another look at your personal finances. Once a month, you get a paycheck from your employer. During the same month, you have a variety of expenses you need to pay. It's not much different than what we saw in the income statement. You need to pay for your housing expenses, clothing and food, and you usually pay for these expenses in cash. It does not need to be cash in the sense that you can touch it and it is in your pocket. But it is cash that you have full access to; for example, your personal bank account. You can also look at your personal cash flow statement as something that measures the actual flow of cash that you have available.

This also explains why there are some important distinctions. If you buy something on credit, you can buy bigger, more expensive things that you might not have the cash for. This could, for instance, be the purchase of a brand new TV. Say that the price is $2,000; you might need to pay only $200 a month for the next ten months. This means that, even though you have something worth $2,000 in your home, in your personal cash flow statement, only $200 would be deducted the following month.

Your monthly cash flow statement may look something like this:

Money in the bank (start of month)	$ 500
Monthly salary	$ 2,500
Housing cost	$ -1,200
Food expenses	$ -400
Birthday present	$ 400
TV installment	$ -200
Other expenses	$ -700
Money in the bank (end of month)	$ 900

Credit considerations are important for all companies too. Companies have numerous daily transactions in which they either obtain credit from a supplier or give credit to a customer. This enables purchases and sales to be made—and that is what you see in the income statement. But the flow of cash occurs later, and that is what the company's cash flow statement tells us.

Although you might have a well-paid job that covers your daily expenses with an adequate margin, you may still experience a tightening in your budget during Christmas and holidays.

Cash flow statements work the same way for companies: they measure how cash is moving in and out of the company. As such, the company can always track how much cash it has, thereby avoiding the unfortunate situation where it has no cash to pay creditors, employees or any other third party. That is not very different to you being more careful at the end of the month when your personal account starts to show a lower level of cash. Cash is indeed king for everyone.

At first glance, the income statement and cash flow statement might seem very similar. In many ways, they are. But the key difference is the income statement is capturing the profit of the business over time, and the cash flow statement is looking at the changes in cash over time. Your personal income statement, for example, might tell me that you made a profit of $20,000 last year, whereas your personal cash flow statement would show me that you kept a $1,000 balance in your checking account throughout the year. I will explain the cash flow statement in much greater detail in Chapter 8.

Chapter 3 A Brief Introduction to Financial Statements

Basic report terminology for the stock investor

There are a few things that are nice to know when you start to learn more about accounting. Financial statements, as we just saw, are separate components that, when combined, are called 10Ks (annual), 10Qs (quarterly) and 8Ks (unscheduled).

To understand this, you must know that the government imposes required reports on publicly traded companies. Every company must file an annual report and a quarterly report that contains the major financial information for the stated time period. The reports that are delivered to the shareholders—typically in shiny folders—are usually less extensive than the reports filed with the government. For this reason, you may prefer to read the reports prepared for the government.

• **10K (Annual Report):** The 10K is the name denoted to the annual accounts that are filed for all major business activities conducted in the last year. Every corporation must file their annual accounts within sixty to ninety days after the fiscal year ends, depending on the size of the business. The annual reports generally cover the company's background along with the mission and vision of the organization. The annual accounts cover the hierarchical structure of the organization, equity holdings, employees' interest, non-controlling interest, subsidiaries, any legal issues faced by the company, the auditors, the control procedures, and executives' remuneration.

The three main financial statements are published with detailed notes on accounts, disclosures and any events that might have occurred after the balance sheet date. Government authorities and investors are likely to be interested in annual accounts because they detail valuable information for analyzing the company's present and future growth prospects.

- **10Q (Quarterly Report):** The quarterly reports produced by the company are called 10Q. These reports are a lot like the 10K but only cover the previous quarter—or last three months. Companies must file their quarterly accounts within forty to forty-five days from the end of the fiscal quarter, depending on the size of the company. The quarterly report is very similar to the annual report, only it's not as encompassing.

- **8K (Current Report Filing):** In addition to the annual and quarterly report requirements, publicly traded companies are also required to file a form that reports any major event that could have an effect on the company's financial position; for example, acquisitions or mergers or any incident that significantly harms the corporation's earning capacity. Major events could also include forms of bankruptcy, sale of a subsidiary, a change in board of directors or a change in the reported fiscal year. Major events such as these are likely to have a large impact on a corporation's earning capacity and therefore companies are required to file a form no later than four days from the date of the event's occurrence.

So what's the point of discussing the 10K, 10Q, and 8K? Well, these reports are important because they hold the keys to solving a very important puzzle: the value puzzle. At the end of the day, our ultimate goal as stock investors is to know the value of each and every stock we buy. You wouldn't buy a house without knowing what it is worth, so why would you buy a business any differently? As said many times before, buying one share is the same as buying the whole business. So if you are buying a business, you need to know its value. Reading these three reports will unlock the door to a company's true value—or intrinsic value.

Chapter 4
The Principles and Rules of Value Investing

Warren Buffett invests according to four simple principles.

1. Vigilant leadership
2. Long-term prospects
3. Stock stability
4. Buy at attractive prices.

One of the greatest strengths of Warren Buffett is his ability to make things simple. As you can see above, his principles are straightforward and easy to remember. As you navigate your way through this book, always keep these four principles at the forefront of your mind. Ensuring that all four are met at all times is paramount to anything else. In order to evaluate these four principles, Buffett uncovers data and qualitative information from the 10K and 10Q reports. As you already learned, these reports are required by the Security Exchange Commission (SEC) and are available to anyone in the public.

When Warren Buffett worked for Benjamin Graham, he was taught a very mathematical way of picking stocks. Although this approach guided Buffett's methodology early on, he slowly deviated from Graham's teachings in a couple different ways. I have provided the framework for understanding those deviations along with subordinate rules for each of the principles. Remember, these nested rules are provided to help you gain a clearer picture of the overarching four principles. The first three principles will have qualitative features and some numbers. The last principle is based on quantitative features and is rooted in mathematics. When applying all four principles together, you'll be meshing the opinions of the artist with the facts of the engineer. Your success is heavily dependent on the understanding of and discovery from both dynamics.

Principle 1—Vigilant leaders

This principle has four subordinate rules that will help you determine whether a company is managed by vigilant leaders. Although numerous other factors exist, these rules can be used as a starting point for your overall assessment.

Rule 1—Low debt
Rule 2—High current ratio
Rule 3—Strong and consistent return on equity
Rule 4—Appropriate management incentives.

Imagine that you are taking the same taxicab to work every day. You can choose between a driver who always keeps the cab within the speed limit, or you can choose a driver who runs red lights and cuts corners. Which kind of driver would you choose? I personally think the latter would be exciting and thrilling, but I would rather choose the first one on a permanent basis. I would like the driver and me to have the same interest. In this situation, the driver would be my agent for ensuring safety.

Warren Buffett feels the same way about management. He knows that management is an agent for him as an owner (or shareholder). This agent should serve his interest at all times; that interest is to make the most of his invested capital. He also knows that vigilant leaders are always on the lookout for danger.

In reality, most management does not act in the interest of the owners. Sometimes they focus more on optimizing their own pay rather than optimizing returns to the shareholders. In other cases, management may have the intention of maximizing the returns to the shareholders, but are taking high risks in doing so. Lastly, many managers simply want to grow their "empire" with the shareholder's retained earnings. The bigger the enterprise, the more credibility their personality—or at least they think. All these situations create less value for you as a shareholder. By the end of this principle, we will discuss some rules that will help you to identify and avoid such managements.

Rule 1—Low debt

Debt is like stepping on the accelerator in your car. If the road ahead is smooth, you will get there faster. But if you find sharp curves or bumps in the road, you will quickly find yourself in trouble.

Debt in investing and personal finances works the same way; for example, you can choose to finance your car either with your own savings or through debt. It may be tempting to borrow money for a car as this enables you to buy a more expensive model. The situation is even more pronounced when buying a house. Most people would never be able to buy a house with cash. Debt is a simple and effective instrument to get what you want faster. As long as you have a stable income that can pay off the mortgage, you should be on easy street.

If you take precautions, there is nothing wrong with accelerating your personal finances. The problems occur if you hit sharp curves and bumps in the road. Though we do not like to think about it, unhappy circumstances happen now and then. People get fired and sometimes people get sick. Many homeowners have found themselves in that unfortunate situation, and ultimately discover how important it is to have minimal debt obligations.

The situation is the same for stock investing. When you buy stock in a company that has a lot of debt, that company's management has decided to accelerate time. They needed to own a particular asset right now in order to earn more business or remain competitive within their industry. When you buy yourself into a company, you own a little part of the company's assets. If the assets are financed with debt, your assets are bought with other people's money. On the one hand, this allows the company to acquire more assets, which is great when times are good. On the other hand, it also increases the risk of the company if demand declines or competition intensifies. Think of debt in the same way you think about a boat traveling on a particular course. Large amounts of debt would look like a cruise liner or oil vessel. Small amounts of debt would look like a tiny speedboat. If both of these boats were traveling in the same direction and speed and suddenly came upon shallow land, think about the maneuverability choices that both captains would face as they try to circumnavigate the obstacle. The cruise liner would obviously be obtuse and slow to react. Its path is pretty much set, with very little room to adjust its course; whereas the speedboat can quickly change course and continue in a different direction. As you can see, we are trying to find companies in the latter category. We want companies that possess flexibility and adaptability for the course ahead. As you already know, business is highly competitive. The course ahead is pliable and constantly changing. Without agility, companies lack longevity.

Out of all the metrics you're going to learn, this one will likely be one of the most important: avoid companies with large amounts of debt.

In investing, one of the tools we have for measuring this risk is called the debt-to-equity (D/E) ratio. This ratio is really easy to understand and apply. For starters, let's calculate your personal D/E ratio right now. This exercise is very similar to the one we did in Chapter 3.

I want you to take a piece of paper and draw a line down the middle, splitting the paper into two halves. On the right side of the page, list all your debs—for example:

House	$200,000 (be sure to only list the amount remaining on your loan)
Car	$10,000
Furniture	$2,000
etc…	

Now on the left side of the page, list all the things you own. Be sure to list the fair market value of each item; for example, your house might be worth $300,000, but your TV might only be worth $50. You don't need to be extremely thorough; simply list the big-ticket items.

Once you've completed both lists, add up the value at the bottom of the left and right columns. On the left side of the page, you have your assets. On the right side of the page, you have your liabilities. In order to determine your equity, you need to take the difference between these two numbers.

Let's say you had $350,000 in assets (left side) and $250,000 in liabilities (right side). The difference between the two numbers is $100,000—that would be your equity. This is what you would have left if you sold all your assets and paid off your creditors.

Now, to determine your debt-to-equity (D/E) ratio, we will simply divide your liabilities (right side), by the equity number you just determined (i.e., $100,000). In the example, the debt to equity would be $250,000 / $100,000. This gives us a D/E of 2.5.

As you intuitively try to understand the importance of this number, try substituting different liabilities into the debt variable to see how the ratio changes; for example, if your debt was very low, the ratio approaches zero. If the debt was really high, the ratio also moves higher. In the end, it's simply a multiple. If your debt is $200,000 and your equity is $100,000, we can quickly say that you have twice as much debt as equity. This is reflected in the D/E ratio as a 2.0. Warren Buffett likes a debt-to-equity ratio of 0.5 or lower. I suggest that you begin investing in companies with low debt. As you become more familiar with investing, you may like to assume more risk and allow companies with slightly more debt into your portfolio. In the end, you're the person assuming the risk for all your decisions, so choose wisely.

Now, as with all ratios, this is just a rule of thumb. Some industries are characterized by low debt-to-equity ratios; while banks, with a core product of debt, typically have higher ratios. You should therefore also consider the industry standard for normal levels of debt.

It is important to understand that a company should not aim to have no debt at all. That is seldom a goal in itself. A company's goal should be the flexibility to enter good projects at all times and withstand any challenges in the market. This is generally achieved when the company sustains a low debt-to-equity ratio of below 0.5.

Rule 2—High current ratio

Do you ever find yourself running low on cash at the end of the month? If you do, you are not alone. A lot of people have well-paid jobs yet still struggle to make ends meet with their personal finances. The question is really not how much they *make*, but how much they *spend*.

Even highly profitable companies face the same challenges. Their product may be great and there might be a high demand for it. But they seem to be short of cash all the time. The problem may very well be that their *current ratio* is too low.

In Chapter 3, I introduced assets and liabilities on the balance sheet. Assets were what the company owned, and liabilities were what the company owed. When we talk about *current* asset, it is something that we expect will turn into cash within the next twelve months. It could be inventory that we expect to sell when the next order is placed. A current liability, on the other hand, is something that we need to pay within the next twelve months. It could be raw materials that we have received from a supplier but haven't yet paid for.

When we compare our current assets and current liabilities, we are actually looking at the current ratio. The formula is very simple and looks like this:

$$\text{Current Ratio} = \text{Current Assets} / \text{Current Liabilities}$$

Warren Buffett generally likes a current ratio above 1.5. That means that he wants his companies to receive $1.5 every time a debt of $1 must be paid within the next twelve months. The idea is straightforward: if a company always receives more cash than it pays out, the company can meet its short-term debt obligations at any time.

When analyzing the annual report, you will see that a high current ratio is typically a sign of a healthy company. If the ratio is below 1, often the company would have to acquire new debt to pay off the existing debt obligations. That only postpones and accumulates problems.

As such, it is also hard to put a strict rule on the current ratio. For most companies, a current ratio of between 1.5 and 2.5 is desirable. A low current ratio may mean that the company has problems meeting their short-term obligations, while a higher current ratio may indicate bad money management due to an inability to collect payment from vendors. Like most things, a balance between both extremes is desirable.

Rule 3—Strong and consistent return on equity

Are you good at first impressions? Do you smile and offer a firm handshake when you meet new people? A company's first impression is their return on equity (ROE). Just as a first impression only gives you a quick snapshot of who the other person is, ROE gives you a snapshot of whether you should invest in the company or not.

In Chapter 3, I introduced the net income: the profit that a company makes for a given year. I also introduced the equity of a company, which is simply the assets subtracted by the liabilities. These two numbers are the basis for the simple formula for ROE:

Return on Equity = Net Income / Shareholders' Equity.

Let's say you had the unique opportunity to purchase a money machine. The machine costs $100,000 to own. The machine is capable of printing $10,000 worth of money every year. This means an investment in the money machine would give you a return on equity of 10%. The cost of the machine is your equity and the profit from the printing is your net income. It's truly that simple.

When you look at stock, you need to view it in a similar light.

Now, let's expand on our example. Let's say we have another opportunity to buy a second money machine. This machine costs $200,000 to own.

Like the first machine, the second machine also prints $10,000 worth of money every year. Based on this new investment, what would our total ROE look like after we buy the second machine?

Return on Equity = Net Income / Shareholders' Equity
Return on Equity = ($10,000 + $10,000) / ($100,000 + $200,000)
Return on Equity = $20,000 / $300,000
ROE = 6.7%

Now, this is very important. We saw our ROE decrease from 10% to 6.7% based on our decision to buy the second money machine. Our decision made the company's performance less efficient compared to the value of the assets we already possessed

To illustrate this important point, let's go back to the spot where we bought the second money machine. Instead of buying the second money machine, let's say we had a competitive offer to buy a hotdog stand instead. The hotdog stand costs $50,000 to own and it produces a $10,000 annual profit. Assuming we purchased the hotdog stand instead of the second money machine, what would our ROE be?

Return on Equity = Net Income / Shareholders' Equity
Return on Equity = ($10,000 + $10,000) / ($100,000 + $50,000)
Return on Equity = $20,000 / $150,000
ROE = 13.3%

As we closely examine the two different paths, we can see how the first option (two money machines) produced a $20,000 profit, and the second option (a money machine and a hotdog stand), also produced a $20,000 profit. Although the profit was the same, the second choice was better because it cost us less to produce the same profit. Our choices from a management standpoint were more efficient with the second path. In short, we produce the same profit with half the equity. This is a great thing because it means we have $150,000 less money tied up. This extra money can now be used to buy more assets; for example, maybe we could purchase another three hotdog stands with the $150,000 difference. Think of the impact that would have on the ROE.

As you can see, the ROE is extremely important because it demonstrates the effectiveness of management's ability to reinvest your profits in the business. Considering most companies retain most of the profits and reinvest the money for you, you'll probably find the ROE one of the most important figures for assessing the performance of your stock. It should come as no surprise that ROE is Warren Buffett's favorite number.

In general, you should look for companies that have had a consistent ROE of above 8% over the last ten years. While it is always hard to give more than a rule of thumb in accounting, a ROE above 8% generally tells you that the company is consistently making a decent profit with the earnings that management retains.

Unfortunately, it is not enough just to check whether the ROE is above or below 8%. For one thing, you should check the trend. You want to look for a ROE that has been steady or even increasing over the last eight to ten years. The reason this is so important is when a company is making a profit, it will generally keep all or some of the capital for future investments. This increases the equity, which is in the denominator of the formula above.

On the other hand, it also means that if the company does not earn a proportionally higher income when earnings are retained and reinvested, the ROE will decline. This is why Warren Buffett places so much emphasis on this key ratio. It captures all the different aspects of how the shareholders' money is employed. It does not matter whether the money has been used on new equipment or the company has paid too much for acquiring a competitor. The net income must follow the investment level to maintain a steady ROE.

That said, you should still think of 8% as a general benchmark. A satisfactory ROE differs across sectors. In the insurance industry, a steady trend of around 8% may be fine, but in the IT industry, it might not be adequate; therefore, after you have checked the trend, you should look at the industry for a comparison.

A major driver behind the validity of ROE is the company's financing structure. As you will recall from Chapter 3, a company can be financed with equity, debt, or a combination of the two. As you will also recall, you should be very cautious about companies with a debt-to-equity ratio of higher than 0.5. If you fail to find companies with minimal debt, you might find yourself in a ROE mirage.

Equity	100	90	80	70	66.6	60	50	40	30	20	10
Debt	0	10	20	30	33.3	40	50	60	70	80	90
Earnings	10	10	10	10	10	10	10	10	10	10	10
D/E	0.00	0.11	0.25	0.43	0.50	0.67	1.00	1.50	2.33	4.00	9.00
ROE	10.0%	11.1%	12.5%	14.3%	15.0%	16.7%	20.0%	25.0%	33.3%	50.0%	100.0%

As you can see from this table, you should look at the value and trend of the ROE with one eye, and the financing structure (or D/E) with the other. So you're probably wondering which number is more important. The answer is that *both* are equally important. Think of debt as your metric for risk and ROE as your metric for return. Warren Buffett's professor, Ben Graham, consistently said to never be attracted to a high return while compromising security. Or, in other words, manage risk first (i.e., D/E), then consider the remaining choices based on yield (i.e., ROE). By choosing a company with a historical D/E of below 0.5, you will most likely end up with companies with lower ROE, but they will likely be more sustainable in the future.

As you have seen, and will continue to see as we move along, accounting ratios such as ROE are subject to a lot of distortion when it comes to a company's true performance. It is therefore important that you look at the long-term historical trends. This will enable you to capture a much more credible view of the company's performance. Simply looking at one year's ROE can be misleading. The key for you is to understand both how net income (or profit) and equity are composed. When you do this, ROE is a great measure to use.

Rule 4—Appropriate management incentives

What do sports stars and stock market investors have in common? They both need trustworthy agents in order to be successful. Imagine a contract for a sports star being drawn up something like this:

The agent receives 10% of the salary for the next contract he mediates.

What do you expect will happen if the agent for the sports star can choose between a high-paying or a low-paying contract? How much do you think it matters to the agent that the sports star signs with a good team versus the highest-paying team?

You guessed it! If the sports star is not paying close attention to the agent's actions, the agent may act in his own self-interest and not the star's. In finance and investing, we call this the "principal agent problem." You, as an investor, are the principal, and you want the management, which is your agent, to act in your interest when running the business.

This is not as easy as it sounds. In the business world, the agent is corporate management. The sports star is you, the owner. The corporate management is working for you—plain and simple. You hired them to run your business. Now, you might not have called them up and personally put them into their job, but if you had enough shares in the business, you might have that ability as the chairman of the board. You see, if all the stockholders got together in an auditorium, they would holistically represent the entire ownership of any given business. Since this is nearly impossible to do, all the shareholders elect a board to represent them. This body of owners is called the board of directors. The board of directors represents the interests and ideas of all the owners—or shareholders. As you might expect, the chairman of the board is the top guy leading the board. If you don't like a particular decision the company has made, you need to coordinate with the members of the board. They will, in turn, voice that concern to the management that's been hired to run the company—i.e., the CEO and his staff. In the end, never forget that you're the guy at the top of the pecking order. You're the owner of the business—the principal.

As we look at this relationship, we can quickly see all the different interests operating simultaneously. The management—or agent—obviously wants to make money for the owners, but there are also other agendas at play; for example, the CEO may want to expand "his" empire. This may result in his decision to purchase new and expensive acquisitions for the company. This may create very little value for the owners compared to the capital needed to grow the size of the business.

What should you do about this as an investor? How can you, as an outsider, see what is going on inside the company? Well, sometimes things are simply outside your purview. Other times, you might see disturbing trends in the financial reports or news articles. In the end, your willingness to dig for information will likely result in a better understanding and ability to understand the management you have (indirectly) hired.

A good place to start is by looking at how management is compensated. Executives are seldom paid only a basic salary. Almost all executives are compensated by a base salary and some kind of bonus package. There is nothing wrong with that, as long as the compensation really does measure performance and incentivize future performance. Sadly, that is sometimes not the case.

Traditionally, compensation packages have been tied to the performance of the stock. For one thing, the stock price in the short run is almost completely random. No one can predict what will happen to the stock price of a single company within a few months. A bear market will punish even the best managers, and a bull market will reward even the worst.

Another, more severe, factor is that compensation based on stock price performance gives management wrong incentives to act truthfully as your agent. Management can actually do a lot to increase the share price in the short term, which is not in your favor as the shareholder. Yes, that is true. A rising stock price for artificial reasons is not good for you as an investor (assuming you want to hold your investments for the long haul like Warren Buffett). Management that artificially inflates earnings in the short term will always account for lower (relative) earnings in the long term—that's why they call it accounting.

If management is giving the incentive to solely focus on the share price, the management is also given the incentive not to pay out dividends, but rather to retain all earnings even though there are no good projects to invest in. Remember that a company's equity or net worth drops when dividends are paid out, simply because there is less cash in the company.

As mentioned before, another thing that can happen when management is given inappropriate incentives is that it starts to focus on the psychology of the market. This means that they give statements and take decisions that often are shortsighted and very risky. One classical example is to set unrealistic goals for the company earnings. The market rewards ambitious goals in the short run, but punishes them in the long run when it becomes clear that they become unrealistic.

If management is compensated by short-term stock price increases, it will have an incentive to do whatever it can to boost company earnings. If the stock price is such a bad measure for management performance, and furthermore gives the wrong incentives to management, why are so many management compensation packages structured in this shortsighted way?

The answer is actually quite simple: the stock price is an easy and transparent measurement stick. The board that draws up the compensation package and policies is often comprised of shareholders who sometimes have a short-term horizon themselves.

So, how should one ideally measure performance and what should you look for when validating whether a company has trustworthy management that will work as your agent? The first thing to do is to look at the notes in the annual report. The accounting rules declare that management's salary must be disclosed. Some companies do whatever they can to distort any information about this. Needless to say, you do not want to invest in these companies. On the other hand, trustworthy companies and management teams go beyond this and disclose the structure of the compensation plans. You want a company that discloses how much the base salary is and how much is variable, and which indicators the management is measured on. Clearly you can't expect a company to disclose that manager X gets $500,000 in an annual base salary and can expect to receive another $300,000 if he manages to increase sales by 2,000 units by the end of next year. That specific information is, and should be, classified.

But you can expect a trustworthy management with high integrity to disclose a management incentive structure that is coherent with your interests as a shareholder. That means that managers are first and foremost rewarded based on performance and long-term goals. Managers should only be rewarded for what they themselves can influence. For most managers, this would include their specific divisions. Only top managers can be expected to be rewarded for the performance of the whole organization. You should also look for rewards for long-term goals. Being an investor and owner with long-term goals, you want your managers to be in line with you; for example, you should look for long-term roadmaps with a variety of objectives to be obtained.

This is an important feature to understand about any organization. If you're looking to own a company for an extended period of time (which I highly encourage), then you'll want to understand the standards and procedures of the management team. You'll be surprised at the variance from one company to the next.

Summing up: Vigilant leaders

1) A debt-to-equity ratio of below 0.5 is preferred. Debt can disrupt even the best businesses because it limits flexibility and agility.

2) To maintain flexibility, you should also make sure that you are getting more cash in than what is going out. This can be measured by the current ratio, which should be at least 1.5.

3) Vigilant leaders also aim to make a decent return on equity (ROE). Above 8% consistently over a period of ten years is a strong indication of great management.

4) Management is your agent. Their one and only task is to give you the most value for your invested capital. Make sure that they have the appropriate monetary incentives to do so.

Principle 2—A company must have long-term prospects

The next principal has two subordinate rules:

Rule 1—Persistent products
Rule 2—Minimize taxes

In some sense, meteorologists, investors and fortune tellers are all in the same line of business: they all try to predict the future. The average stock investor aims to determine how the demand for a certain product will develop. Even more courageous, investors, for example in high-tech industries, even try to determine the demand and market potential for innovative products they can't even buy yet. Value investors maybe more practical, but the goal is the same. They also want to know which products will sell in the future; however, they put more emphasis on the company's current ability to earn. Those earnings potentially are then applied to future years to determine an estimated return on investment through the long haul. The reason for this is quite simple: value investors try to minimize taxes by owning outstanding businesses that remain stable over a lifetime.

Rule 1—Persistent products

Do you own a smartphone? If yes, is it an iPhone or an Android? The answer is not that important, but the question is. When you read this, perhaps iPhones and Androids are no longer in production. Sometime from now, people may even wonder what a smartphone is—and that is really what this rule is all about.

As a value investor, you don't want to jump in and out of the market all the time. As we will examine in the next rule, taxes and broker fees make this short-term thinking too expensive. Instead, you want to invest in a "persistent" product, a product that will not change in the next thirty years. If we return to the example with the smartphones, I find it highly unlikely that consumers will be using the smartphones we know today in thirty years. That does not mean that Apple cannot continue to be a profitable innovative company in the future; it simply means that products like iPhones are more unpredictable compared to other products. This opinion leaves me skeptical about highly technical stocks and businesses as long-term ventures

Ben Graham would constantly stress to his students that speculation was reliant on a change in future results, whereas investing was not. As Apple looks to their future profits, therefore, it will undoubtedly be reliant on their ability to develop a new technology and product—whereas a company like Coke is not reliant on changing their future product. This is what Graham was talking about.

I can't give you a tool to determine with certainty which products will be used thirty years from now. But what I can do is give you Warren Buffett's guideline for products that he avoids as investment objects. It is simply this:

"Will the Internet change the way we use the product?"

Now, this guideline may be too simple to capture the future demands of all products. But the message is clear. A value investor is interested in persistent products that do not change due to technology. To show the power of this guideline, let us look at Coke. People have been drinking Coke for more than a century. We drank Coke before Apple invented iPhones and Intel produced microchips. And I am sure that we will still drink Coke when iPhones are outdated and microchips have been replaced with something even more advanced.

Technology has never changed the way we drink Coke or soft drinks, by and large. People have always liked sugar and will continue to do so. That has nothing to do with the stock market; it is a biological fact. Now, there might be a variety of reasons of why you do not want to own shares in Coke, but I am sure that soft drinks not having long-term prospects is not one of them.

When considering a new investment, you should aim to easily determine whether technology will significantly change the demand or use of the product. If it can, you should maybe consider an alternate investment object—or assume the risks associated with such a venture and be prepared for its consequences/rewards.

For instance, people have always had the need for communicating with each other. We used to write letters, and before that we used telegraphs. There is no reason to believe that there will be less communication in the future; however, whether this communication will continue on one of Apple's products is hard to predict. Value investing is about finding persistent and predictable products with long-term prospects. A product that has been here for thirty years and can be expected to be here for at least another thirty years is a good place to start your search for valuable companies.

Rule 2—Minimize taxes

Do you know the formula for getting rich? It is not a secret formula known only to the wealthy. One side of the equation is to maximize your income. The more money you make, the more money you can set aside for future investment and consumption. We often think a lot about this side of the equation. But the other side of the equation is just as important—if not more so: you should minimize your expenses.

I am not talking about remembering to turn off the lights when leaving your home, or taking the bus instead of the car. I am talking about one of your biggest expenses in personal finances: taxes. Few people notice it because they only look at the bottom of their pay slip, but taxes are a major expense in every household.

In investing, taxes are equally a problem for profit maximization. If you are like me, your goal with value investing is to establish a new source of income outside your daily job. By minimizing your tax, you indirectly improve your return on investments. Luckily, minimizing taxes on capital gains is very easy to do.

The following table shows the current American tax bracket for 2014. Don't worry if you do not live in America; this example is applicable for any investor. In most countries, the tax system is similar to that in America: it rewards value investors who are in the game for the long haul, and punishes day traders who aren't creating value but are simply trying to make a quick buck.

2014 Short and Long-term Capital Gains tax for filing as a single person		
Ordinary Income brackets	Short-Term Capital Gains Tax	Long-Term Capital Gains and dividend Tax
$0 to $9,075	10%	0%
$9,076 to $36,900	15%	0%
$36,901 to $89,350	25%	15%
$89,351 to $186,350	28%	15%
$186,351 to $405,100	33%	15%
$405,101 to $406,750	35%	15%
More than $406,750	39.6%	20%

Short-term capital gain < 1 year of holding

Your tax rate on capital gains is determined by your ordinary income tax rate; for example, if your ordinary income is $100,000 you would still pay 28% in tax if you make a short-term capital gain, but if you hold on to the stock for more than a year, you would only pay 15% tax on the gain. The tax system favors the value investor over the average investor. If you ever wondered why Warren Buffett's holding period is forever, this is why.

In addition to a lower tax rate, you must also realize that this tax is only paid if you decide to sell the stock; for example, if you hold on to a stock for twenty years, the value of the stock can compound with no friction of personal taxes each year. You only pay this tax when you decide to sell the position after twenty years. On the other hand, if you owned a bunch of different stocks within the same twenty years and always sold your position within a year's timeframe, you would pay the high tax rate every single year.

Let me illustrate the tax effect in this generic example.

You invest $50,000 in a 10% investment and hold for 20 years

Year 1	$55,000		Year 11	$142,656
Year 2	$60,500		Year 12	$156,921
Year 3	$66,550		Year 13	$172,614
Year 4	$73,205		Year 14	$189,875
Year 5	$80,526		Year 15	$208,862
Year 6	$88,578		Year 16	$229,749
Year 7	$97,436		Year 17	$252,724
Year 8	$107,179		Year 18	$277,996
Year 9	$117,897		Year 19	$305,795
Year 10	$129,687		Year 20	$336,375

Before Taxes:	$336,375
After 15% taxes on the gains:	$293,419
Total tax Paid:	$42,956

This table shows the growth of a $50,000 investment and how it compounded over a 20-year period. At the end of this period, the investor pays tax only once—at 15% on the growth. The investment turns into $293,419 after taxes. The assumption is the principal grew at a steady 10% increase every year.

You invest $50,000 in a 10% investment and sell each year

Year	Amount	Year	Amount
Year 1	$53,600	Year 11	$107,427
Year 2	$57,459	Year 12	$115,162
Year 3	$61,596	Year 13	$123,453
Year 4	$66,031	Year 14	$132,342
Year 5	$70,785	Year 15	$141,870
Year 6	$75,882	Year 16	$152,085
Year 7	$81,345	Year 17	$163,035
Year 8	$87,202	Year 18	$174,774
Year 9	$93,481	Year 19	$187,357
Year 10	$100,212	Year 20	$200,847

Final Growth after 28% taxes every year:	$200,847
Taxes Paid:	$58,663

In this table, you will see how a day trader in the 28 % tax bracket experiences 10% annual growth. Since he is trading between different stocks, he will pay the short-term capital gains rate every year. What is interesting about this example is that the return he got from his stocks was exactly the same as that of the value investor (10% per year), but he ends up with much less due to the taxes paid. If we compare the value investor's results with those of the day trader, they look like this:

Comparison of a hold strategy to a buy-sell strategy

Hold Strategy After 15% Taxes	Buy-Sell Strategy After 28% Taxes
$293,419	**$200,847**
Taxes Paid **$42,956**	Taxes paid **$58,663**

What is really interesting is that the taxes paid are not that different. The day trader has only paid $15,707 more in tax than the value investor. Still, the value investor ends up with $92,572 more than the day trader. As you can see, the friction of an annual tax expense diminishes the compounding effect. As a result, the day trader is consistently paying higher taxes of a smaller amount—and he's doing a lot more work too.

This example really shows the power behind Warren Buffett's second principle of investing. By investing in companies with long-term prospects, you maintain as much return on your investment as possible, by minimizing your taxes.

Summing up: A company must have long-term perspectives

1) Persistent demand for the products or services is a crucial characteristic of Warren Buffett's second principle. Warren Buffett's favorable holding period is *forever*.

2) Tax is one of your biggest expenses as an investor. Let your investment compound and grow for a long period of time before the government gets their share. You'll be rewarded by higher relative returns and lower tax rates.

Principle 3—A company must be stable and understandable

Rule 1—Stable book value growth from the owner's earnings

Rule 2—Sustainable competitive advantage (moat)

If you think that Warren Buffett has become rich by finding new and exciting companies with products that the world has never seen, you only need to take a look at his portfolio to be proven wrong.

According to Warren Buffett, one key element in his strategy is to only invest in companies that are stable and understandable. If a company is not stable, Buffett cannot reduce his risk and value the company properly. If he cannot understand the company, he cannot determine whether the business is profitable now and will be in the future. In fact, investing in stable companies might have been the most important rule that Benjamin Graham taught Warren Buffett for minimizing risk in an investment.

In addition to finding a stable business, Warren Buffett also talks about the idea of staying within your "circle of competences." Buffett is well aware that there are a lot of businesses in this world that he simply doesn't understand. He therefore chooses to stay within his circle of competences, which basically means only doing what he is good at. In this sense, it is less important whether you know ten or a thousand businesses and sectors, as long as you stick with what you know. As Buffett puts it: "At the Olympics, if you run the hundred meters well, you don't have to do the shot-put."

Ultimately, you also need to understand the company because you would otherwise not know when to sell or buy the stock again. If you understand the company, you will understand the fundamentals that drive the profit, thereby also understanding the company's competitive edge.

Chapter 4 The Principles and Rules of Value Investing

Rule 1—Stable book value growth from the owner's earnings

I love to read about this year's "must have" gadget. I personally think it is amazing what new innovative companies emerge each year. The funny thing is, I usually don't know about the company before reading the article, and I seldom hear about them ever again. But new and exciting companies are generally not stable, and stability is exactly what we should be looking for if we want to follow Buffett's simple principles.

So how do we measure the stability of a stock? In the most simple form, I suggest that you look at the stability and growth of book value and earnings per share. This is not only because Warren Buffett says that the changes in book value are similar to the changes in intrinsic value, but because it explains two very important aspects of investing. It shows that book value growth comes from earnings, and it explains the importance of *owner's earnings.*

Let's first look at a generic example of book value growth from earnings. As you probably remember, the equity (or book value) of a company is really the shareholders' money. A company should always aim to increase the wealth of its shareholders, which means that either the company's assets must increase or its liabilities must decrease. These changes must come from earnings.

Let's assume that you just started a sandwich shop and you financed it with $1,000 of your own money and $500 from the bank. Your balance sheet would look like this at the start of the year:

Assets	1,500	Equity	1,000
		Liabilities	500

	Assets	1,500
—	-Liabilities	500
	Equity	1,000

Chapter 4 The Principles and Rules of Value Investing

You are making great sandwiches and by the end of the year, you have achieved a $100 profit. This $100 can either be used to buy new assets, such as a new refrigerator, or you can pay off your debt to the bank. Let's see what happens in each of these situations. First, you employ the $100 as a new asset:

Assets	1,600	Equity	1,100
		Liabilities	500

Assets	1,600
-Liabilities	500
Equity	1,100

As you can see in the example above, the $100 is added to the assets, which in turn increases the owners' wealth, which is reflected in the equity. Instead of purchasing a new asset, you could also pay off the $500 of liabilities. Let's say you would rather use the $100 to pay back some of the loan. In that case, your balance would look like this:

Assets	1,500	Equity	1,100
		Liabilities	400

Assets	1,500
-Liabilities	400
Equity	1,100

What we see from this example is that if we need to increase equity, the company needs to produce earnings. Whether we use those earnings to buy assets such as a refrigerator or pay off some of our bank loan, it will be equally reflected in the equity.

Finally, let's see an example of how the payment of a dividend will impact the owner's earnings. A dividend is a portion of the income that is returned to the owners in the form of a cash payment. Say that $25 of the $100 is paid out as a dividend. The remaining $75 remains in the company's cash accounts. When you look at your balance sheet, it looks like this:

Assets	1,575	Equity	1,075
		Liabilities	500

Assets	1,575
-Liabilities	500
Equity	1,075

The example above demonstrates the application of owner's earnings. Here, $25 of the original $100 goes back to the owner in the form of a cash dividend. The remaining $75 is retained in the company for future growth and *may* become owner's earnings if it is deployed wisely. If you're wondering what would constitute a wise use of the retained earnings (the $75), simply look at the company's historical Return on Equity (ROE). That will give you a good idea of what management has previously done with the money they have retained. It is extremely important to find a company that demonstrates a consistent earnings capacity, book value growth, and a stable and respectable ROE over numerous years, not just a few.

So let's return to the original sandwich shop scenario and see whether it fulfills Warren Buffett's stability rule.

Assets	1,500	Equity	1,000
		Liabilities	500

Assets	1,500
-Liabilities	500
Equity	1,000

In this example, I have decided to split your sandwich shop into 100 shares resulting in a book value of $10 ($1,000/100) per share. Remember, book value is nothing more than equity per share. I have assumed that the company has reinvested the retained earnings appropriately, therefore the profits continue to grow. This profit growth (or earnings growth) is reflected in a steady earnings per share (EPS) increase over time. This is extremely important: If the company retains earnings (reflected in book value growth), there should be a corresponding growth in future earnings (reflected in EPS growth).

A quick and easy way to check if this is happening is to ensure that the return on equity (ROE) remains constant or even grows. If you look at the graph below, you'll notice that the ROE remains constant as the book value and EPS grow proportionally. As you recall, the ROE is what the owners get in return for the capital that's retained in the company. As investors, we really want this number to be consistent and stable.

Years	EPS	Dividend	Book Value	ROE
Now			$10.00	
1	$1.00	$0.20	$10.80	9.3%
2	$1.20	$0.22	$11.78	10.2%
3	$1.40	$0.24	$12.94	10.8%
4	$1.50	$0.26	$14.18	10.6%
5	$1.50	$0.28	$15.40	9.7%
6	$1.70	$0.30	$16.80	10.1%
7	$1.80	$0.32	$18.28	9.8%
8	$2.10	$0.34	$20.04	10.5%
9	$2.10	$0.36	$21.78	9.6%
10	$2.40	$0.38	$23.80	10.1%

EPS	$16.70		
Dividends		$2.90	
Owners' earnings			$13.80

If we plot this into a graph, it will look like this:

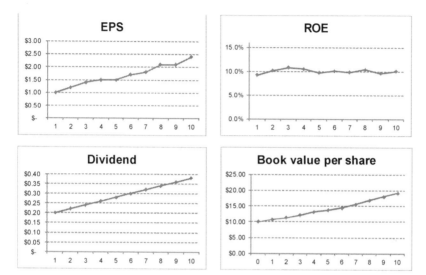

As you can see, you can almost fit a perfect trend line through the ten years for the figures. This is really what value investors are looking for. Because the stock is stable, the value investor has a better chance at predicting future earnings and performance by applying a trend line.

Of course, history does not always repeat itself. Warren Buffett has said, "If past history is all there was to the game, the richest people would be librarians." But, Warren Buffett acknowledges that a stable and understandable company is the basis for minimizing risk and setting expectations for potential performance. In an effort to help you determine the stability of a company, we have created a graphing tool at the BuffettsBooks.com website that allows you to plot ten years' worth of data for any given company. The graphing tool has 6 inputs: EPS, ROE, Dividend Rate, Book Value, Debt/Equity, and the Current Ratio. The specific Web address for accessing the tool is:

http://www.buffettsbooks.com/intelligent-investor/stocks/stock-stability.html

When you arrive at the address, you'll see there are two videos to help you understand how to use the graphing tool.

Although other metrics are also important in determining whether a company is stable and predictable, these criteria are definitely a great starting point. When the numbers check out and stability metrics are fulfilled, we can go on to the qualitative approach. Warren Buffett says, "Valuing a business is part art and part science."

We will now turn to the art of investing.

Rule 2—Sustainable competitive advantage (moat)

When Warren Buffett describes the idea of having a competitive advantage in business, he likens it to a moat around a castle. Enemy businesses will try to conquer your castle if you don't have a moat. Preferably, he would like an honest and hardworking duke to govern that castle—but all wonderful businesses have moats.

While moats can be identified, they are different from one company to another. A company like Coca-Cola has a great moat due to its enormous brand value, whereas a company like Wal-Mart has a wide moat due to its cost structure. Wal-Mart buys on such large volume that it can buy products from its suppliers at a cheaper price than its competitors.

If the moat is wide enough, it is hard—if not impossible—to conquer the castle. The idea is simple: the sustainable competitive advantage cannot be duplicated by competitors; hence the business will keep pouring money into the owners' pockets. If I sold strawberries from a stand, you could set up a similar business right next to mine. But can you duplicate Coca-Cola's brand, or Wal-Mart's cost structure? That is the *moat*.

So far, we have provided a variety of different quantifiable guidelines for Warren Buffett's principles to investing. With competitive advantage, this is not so simple. You can't find anywhere in the financial reports that a moat has increased from 8 to 10. Such a metric does not exist. I urge you to never buy a company that does not have moat. We know that Warren Buffett's second rule is only to invest in long-term prospects, and that goes hand in hand with finding a company that has a unique competitive advantage. A company with no moat will be outmatched over time by competitors, no matter how persistent the demand is for its products and services.

Determining a company's moat is a qualitative process. The things that can create moats in one industry are not the same as those in another industry. In general, I would say that if you cannot see a company's moat, there are two reasons: the first is because it is not there; the second is that you do not sufficiently understand the company. In either case, you'll assume a lot of risk if you invest in the company and you don't understand its competitive advantage. Between all the very specific moats in industries, I would emphasize the following three:

1. Intangible assets such as brands and patents are one type of moat. Disney is an example. It is a strong brand and almost everyone in the world recognizes it. To demonstrate this idea, Warren Buffett uses the example of a mom picking up a movie for her kids on her way home from work. The Disney movie is $1 more expensive than another choice, and she does not know the quality of either of the movies. Which movie would she choose? The Disney movie of course! People identify good things happening with Disney, and that is a hard moat to compete against.

2. Low cost is another type of moat. Every retailer in the world buys goods from suppliers, and since the difference between cost and price is the profit, the retailer will do whatever possible to buy from its suppliers at the lowest cost. Wal-Mart has a wide moat around its business, as it can buy at quantities and prices that competitors can't match.

3. High switching costs—or "stickiness" as Warren Buffett refers to it—is another type of moat. If there is one company with high switching costs, it must be Microsoft Windows. It is very hard to find computers that do not run on Microsoft Windows. It is not about whether there is any better operating system out there. Most people will not bother with the hassle of changing, because they do not want to re-learn the new system. Anyone who invents a new system will have a tough time conquering the operating system's market.

Summing up: A company must be stable and understandable

1) Finding a company that is stable and understandable is paramount because it reduces risk. In the end, we are trying to determine the value of a company (or stock). This can only be accomplished with minimal risk if we can reasonably assess and predict the direction of the company's future earnings.

2) By only investing in companies with a durable competitive advantage, you also reduce long-term risks. A moat can come in the form of intangibles, low-cost structures, and high switching costs (or stickiness).

Principle 4—Buy at attractive prices

Every kid has heard the old saying about a bird in the hand being worth two birds in the bush. Warren Buffett likes to use this same analogy when he talks about investing. Because what *is* investing, really? Isn't it just the decision about whether one dollar today is better than two dollars tomorrow?

Warren Buffett has never publicly disclosed a formula or model for buying undervalued stocks. Still, Warren Buffett is a generous man, and through his shareholders' letters he has revealed the fundamentals of his valuation techniques.

In an effort to keep things as simple as possible, I have developed multiple calculators that incorporate the ideas from Buffett's numerous letters and articles. These calculators will help you determine the intrinsic value of stocks that fulfill the first three principles.

Before we discuss the calculations, I will first present other factors that also apply to finding stocks at attractive prices.

> Rule 1—Keep a wide margin of safety to the intrinsic value
> Rule 2—Low price-earnings ratio
> Rule 3—Low price-to-book ratio
> Rule 4—Set a safe discount rate
> Rule 5—Buy undervalued stocks—Determining intrinsic value
> Rule 6—The right time to sell your stocks

Rule 1 - Keep a wide margin of safety to the intrinsic value

How would you go about building a bridge if you knew that 10,000-pound trucks would be driving over that bridge every day? Would you build the bridge to withstand the pressure of 10,001 pounds? No; you would probably build the bridge to withstand at least 15,000 pounds, and preferably a lot more.

Margin of safety was first introduced by Warren Buffett's professor and mentor Benjamin Graham. It is a very simple, yet powerful, concept for any value investor to understand. If you evaluate a stock to be worth $100, it makes very little sense to buy it at $99. For one thing, you may be completely wrong in your assessment of the stock's value and a margin of $1 leaves very little room for error. On top of the risk you assume, it will be equally hard to make an adequate profit from the stock. Sure, the stock may perform 8-10% a year on average, but you miss out on the extra return you gain from buying an undervalued stock as it returns to its fair value.

When you hear the term "margin of safety," you might think that you have read something along these lines earlier in this book. You are correct! In the first chapter I introduced you to Mr. Market. He was our highly unstable friend with huge mood swings that showed up at our door every day with new prices to buy and sell stocks. He is the reason the stock price does not always follow the company's *intrinsic value*. Remember that the intrinsic value is the company's real or fair value, regardless of what the stock price is. The margin of safety is the difference between the share price and the intrinsic value.

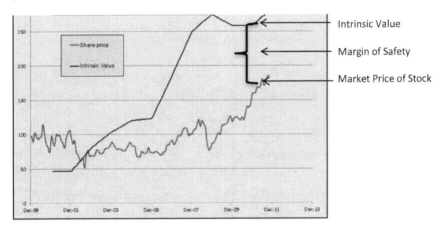

Just as with the example of the bridge, you will want to have as wide a margin of safety as possible. How much you want is based on your desires: if you understand the business and the risks associated with ownership, you will definitely be able to have a narrower margin of safety. It is hard to put an exact number on the margin of safety, as the decision to buy a stock is always dependent on the other alternative choices. If a margin of safety is 30% on one stock, it may look tempting, but if you have the option to buy another great business (of equal risk) with a 50% discount, you would go for that one instead.

Rule 2—Low price-earnings ratio

One of the most basic valuation techniques is the price-earnings ratio (P/E). P/E is so popular with analysts because it gives a quick answer to the one question that all investors keep asking: "How big a return can I get from my investment right now?"

Imagine that you have the opportunity to buy a juice stand at the price of $1,000. Naturally, you would ask the current owner how much profit he made last year. Say that he made $100. Now you have the input to calculate the P/E:

$$\text{Market Price for the company} / \text{Net Income} = \text{P/E}$$

$$\$1,000 / \$100 = 10 = \text{P/E}$$

Since this number is a ratio, we must always remember that the denominator (or number on the bottom of the fraction) is always 1; therefore, a P/E ratio of 10 is actually a 10/1 ratio. This means that every ten dollars of price towards the stock should give you one dollar of earnings (for one year). So if we want to understand this relationship as a percentage, we need to look at the inverse of it—or in other words, the E/P ratio. By taking the inverse of the P/E, we get a percentage yield; for example, the previous situation had a P/E of 10. Therefore 1/10 = 10%. That's the annual yield. Let's try it again but with a different P/E ratio. If you negotiated a lower price of $800 for the juice stand and the business still produced the same earnings, you would have a P/E of: $800/$100 = 8. Or a return of 1/8 = 12.5%. As you can see, a low P/E is preferable to a high P/E.

When you hear that a company has a P/E of 10, this is what the commotion is about. You will often see that the P/E is constantly changing throughout a year. That is very natural. Remember that the share price changes every day, which means the P/E will change every day. When you read financial news, it does not cover juice stands, but rather individual shares. Don't be confused by this; the mechanism is the same whether the price of the company is divided into single shares or you're valuing the entire company. So let's take this simple scenario and add more variables. We said the juice stand was valued at $1,000 for the entire business. Now, let's divide the business into a hundred equal pieces—or shares, if you will. When we divide the business into a hundred shares, each share is now worth $10. Now, the same division occurs for the earnings. If you remember the earnings for the whole business (or net income) was $100, therefore the earnings per share (EPS) is $100/100 = $1 per share. In the previous example, we found the P/E ratio for the entire business. Now we are going to find the P/E for an individual share.

$$\text{Market Price per share} / \text{Earnings per share (EPS)} = \text{P/E}$$
$$\$10/\$1 = 10$$

As you can see, the P/E for the entire company is the same number for one share.

As we have seen in this example, it would be safe to conclude that we want to invest in companies that have low P/E ratios. Why pay a higher price for a single $1 of earnings when you don't have to?

Unfortunately, investing is not that simple. The P/E ratio is simply a current snapshot in time. It looks at the company's present performance in order to determine the value of its future performance. This is often a dangerous path if you fail to consider the other variables.

As you might suspect, a lot of things can happen to the juice stand. The weather that summer may be bad or another juice stand may open right next to ours. Basically, we can't be sure of the $100 in earnings the following years.

Many investors have faced the same dilemma, and therefore they turn to a notion called "forward P/E" instead. The idea behind this is that it uses the projected earnings instead of the past/present earnings. Typically, these future estimations are based on the average estimates of analysts.

So, if we have decided to look at the forward P/E for our juice stand, we might estimate that we could make $200 in earnings. Our forward P/E would therefore be $1,000 / $200 = 5. While this looks more attractive, it also shows that a forward P/E to some extent is a matter of guesswork and opinion.

Warren Buffett is a conservative investor. He suggests that you buy stocks with a P/E ratio below 15—or, in other words, the return should at the very least be 6.67% (which is 1/15) annually. He does not buy into hopes and dreams and he does not think he can spot the new Microsoft. Instead, he buys into a company that is already making a decent profit compared to the price he pays.

Furthermore, Warren Buffett is well aware that earnings can be unstable. In the example of the juice stand, you saw how an increase in the estimated earnings dramatically changed the P/E when we used $200 of earnings instead of the original $100. He therefore places great emphasis on the stability of earnings. Stability is the basis for every valuation technique because it minimizes variability and risk.

Rule 3—Low price-to-book ratio

Another simple valuation technique is the price-to-book ratio (P/B). Let me give you a simple example: say that you pay $10,000 for a car (the price); you will now have an asset worth $10,000 (the book value). The P/B would be 1 in this situation.

For businesses, the principle is the same, though the company might own more assets and have divided the ownership into shares. Here is the simple formula:

Price-to-Book Value Ratio = Market Price per share / Book Value per share

As you will recall, we first introduced equity in Chapter 3. You saw the following figures:

Assets		Liabilities	
Car	$ 20,000	Equity	$ 38,000
Home	$ 150,000	Car debt	$ 15,000
Furniture	$ 3,000	Mortgage	$ 120,000
	$ 173,000		$ 173,000

Equity is what the company owns (asset) subtracted by what the company has borrowed (liability). As equity and book value are the same, Price to Book value or P/B also measures how much the investor pays for every $1 of the company's equity. So let's demonstrate this idea with an example. Looking at the $38,000 of equity from the chart above, let's turn it into a P/B ratio. Let's assume that this company is broken down into 100 shares. Based on that number, we know that the book value would be $380 per share (the math is $38,000/100 shares). We also need to assume a market price for one share, so let's use $570 per share. In order to calculate the P/B ratio, we will simply conduct the following math: P/B = $570/$380 = 1.5. As you can see, the ratio has no units. So what does 1.5 mean?

This means that if the P/B is 1.5, you pay a market price of $1.5 for every $1 of equity on the company's books. Anytime you do this calculation, the last part of the sentence will always be $1 of equity; for example, if the P/B was 5, you would say that you're paying $5.0 for every $1 of equity on the company's books. As you can quickly see, a higher ratio is less exciting because it means you're paying more money to own less equity. If the ratio is below 1, like .50, that means you're paying 50 cents for every $1 of equity.

Now, you might immediately come to the conclusion that the lowest P/B ratio on the market is going to give you the best value, but that would be a bad assumption. To demonstrate what I mean, let's assume you have an opportunity to purchase a company that has a P/B of 0.50. Although you're purchasing the equity of the business at a severe discount, you must also ask yourself, "What's behind the equity." When you ask that question, you might find out that the company manufactures analog TV antennas. As you think about the demand for this 1970 product, you might also realize that the company hasn't made a profit in the last four years. None of that is going to be reflected in the simple P/B ratio of 0.50. You need to dig deeper in order to see the product and/or earnings.

Now, this doesn't mean that every company with a low P/B is a dying company. In fact, during depressed markets, you'll often find many great companies (that still have strong profits) trade below their book value. Your job is to get the whole picture—don't just look at the P/B ratio, you need to compare it to the company's earnings, ROE, and debt (to name a few) all at the same time.

Warren Buffett's mentor Benjamin Graham would try to find companies that had a P/B ratio of below 1.5 as a threshold for indicating value. Although you can go above this limit, just ensure you understand the risks of paying such a high premium for ownership. Just as Warren Buffett likes to buy himself into a decent part of the profit at a low price, he also wants a part of the equity at a low price. If you decide to buy a company with a high P/B, one of the best ways to minimize your exposure to risk is to ensure the company has a large moat—or durable competitive advantage.

Rule 4—Set a safe discount rate

So let's start talking about determining the intrinsic value of a stock. To find the value of any stock, a discount rate must always be determined. Let me provide an example from my personal life: I once had a discussion with my children about money. I asked them some simple questions: "Would you rather have a dollar today, or two dollars tomorrow?" They responded, "Two dollars tomorrow." I then asked, "Would you like to have a dollar today or two dollars next week?" They responded, with a little hesitation, "Two dollars next week."

Trying to reach their breaking point, I asked, "Would you like to have a dollar today or two dollars next year?" They quickly replied, "I want the dollar right now—and stop asking me silly questions."

Although the questioning seemed a little annoying at the time, the purpose was very profound. A dollar today has a completely different value than a dollar tomorrow. So you might be wondering, how can I compare the value of future dollars and present dollars? The answer is by using a discount rate.

By using a discount rate, an investor can take future dollars (or expected dollars) and turn them into present dollars. The beauty of this approach is an investor can take a business's estimated future cash flows and discount them back to today's value. This approach allows investors like Warren Buffett to estimate that company XYZ is worth $100—even though it might be trading for $80. That $100 value is called the *intrinsic value*, or *real value*.

So what discount rate should you use?

Well, the answer to that question depends on your tolerance for risk. Let's say you believe a particular investment is extremely risky. Because this investment is so risky, you will want a very large return. Let's use an extreme example and say you want a 50% return on your money annually because the risk is so high. In this case, your discount rate would be 50%.

On the opposite side of the spectrum, let's talk about a low-risk investment. What should your minimal acceptable return be? Warren Buffett's opinion is that no investment should yield a lower return than a federally issued bond. The reason he holds this opinion is because the Federal Reserve can simply print more money in order to fulfill its interest obligations; therefore, if a ten-year bond has a 3% return, the investor should never discount a ten-year investment decision lower than 3% annually.

When using a discount rate, its higher or lower value will drastically change the intrinsic value of an asset. In short, a higher discount rate produces a lower intrinsic value, whereas a lower discount rate produces a higher intrinsic value. But don't let this confuse you. Let me demonstrate what I'm talking about.

Let's say we are interested in buying a company called XYZ. We believe that company XYZ is going to produce $100 of cash flow (or profit) over the next ten years. Therefore, at the end of ten years, you'll have $100 of cash in your hand. Now, what would you be willing to pay *today* for that $100, ten years from now?

In order to solve that generic question, let's start with a basic time-value of money equation.

PV = present value or intrinsic value today

FV = future value

i = discount rate

n = number of years

$$FV = PV(1+i)^n$$

Let's first solve the equation for the PV (or intrinsic value):

$$PV = \frac{FV}{(1+i)^n}$$

Now that we have our equation ready, let's demonstrate how the intrinsic value of company XYZ changes with the two different discount rates (3% and 50%). We will start with 3%.

$$PV = \frac{FV}{(1+i)^n}$$

$$PV = \frac{\$100}{(1+.03)^{10\ years}}$$

$$PV = \$74.41$$

So here's what that means: if you could buy company XYZ for $74.41 today, you'll earn a 3% return annually for the next ten years. Remember, owning XYZ will put $100 in your hand at the end of ten years.

Now, let's do the same thing for the 50% discount rate.

$$PV = \frac{FV}{(1+i)^n}$$

$$PV = \frac{\$100}{(1+.5)^{10\ years}}$$

$$PV = \$1.73$$

Wow, you weren't expecting that, were you? So here's what this means: if you could buy company XYZ for $1.73 today, you'll earn a 50% return annually for the next ten years—assuming company XYZ can actually produce the $100 of cash flow we estimated.

Remember, in both scenarios (3% or 50%), the end result was the same: you would have $100 in your hand after ten years. The difference is, the 3% rate was used if the investor was comfortable with the expectation of the company actually producing $100 of earnings during the next ten years. With this discount rate, the investor would be willing to pay a higher price for the investment—i.e., the price was $74.41. On the other hand, a 50% rate was used if the investor was uncomfortable with the expectation of the company being able to produce $100 of earnings during the next ten years. In this case, the investor wants to pay a very low price to compensate for the high risk of ownership. At a 50% discount rate, the intrinsic value was a low $1.73 for the investment.

So you're probably still asking, "What discount rate should I use?"

Well, let's flip that question on its head and look at it from a different perspective. Instead, let's determine what the discount rate is. One thing we must remember is that Mr. Market is always offering us a new price for company XYZ. Because we have a market price, we can determine the current discount rate or potential rate of return.

In order to solve this problem, let's rearrange our formula to solve for i.

$$FV = PV(1+i)^n$$

$$i = \sqrt[n]{\frac{FV}{PV}} - 1$$

Now, let's assume that company XYZ is trading on the stock market for $60 a share. Is that a good price based on the cash flow we expect to receive ($100 at the end of ten years)? Well, let's find out what kind of return that will give us annually—or in other words, what discount rate gives us that $60 market price. With this new knowledge (of the market price, or selling price), we can determine our expected yield.

$$i = \sqrt[10]{\frac{\$100}{\$60}} - 1$$

$$i = 5.2\%$$

Now for the big question: is a 5.2% return a sufficient growth on your money for the risk you assume in owning company XYZ? Considering a federal bond is providing a 3% return, you might determine the extra return from company XYZ is not worth the risk. Others might disagree. More importantly, there might be other investment opportunities that could produce a larger return with less risk. These decisions are the definition of opportunity cost. This is what the discount rate is all about.

At the start of this section, you'll remember the questions I asked my children about the time value of money. At a certain point in time, my children, unknowingly, discounted the future cash flow at a rate that made them choose the present dollar over the future dollars. Smart investors understand this process like the backs of their hands.

As we move into the next section, you'll find the calculation for intrinsic value has more parts. The example in this section was to provide a foundation for what a discount rate is and how it's used to compare opportunity costs. The calculation used in this section was an abbreviated approach for demonstration purposes; you'll want to use the advice given in the following rule for determining the intrinsic value.

Rule 5—Buy undervalued stocks—Determining intrinsic value

So far we have seen basic valuation techniques like P/E and P/B which provide a snapshot in time of whether a stock may be undervalued. Determining the intrinsic value of a company is a more laborious process, but it's likely to produce more accurate results and estimates.

Warren Buffett says, "Intrinsic value can be defined simply: It is the discounted value of the cash that can be taken out of a business during its remaining life."

So as we look at that quote, it has two main parts; a discount rate and an estimate of future cash flows. So let's learn some techniques for determining both of those components.

The first thing you'll learn about determining the intrinsic value of a company is that different techniques exist. At the end of the day, any calculation for determining a company's future cash flows is going to have numerous assumptions. In this book, we are going to discuss two different intrinsic value calculations so you have the flexibility to choose which approach you prefer. The first calculation is called a discount cash flow calculation. The second calculation is a variant of the discount cash flow calculation and it values stocks similarly to fixed income bonds. Although both approaches might sound a little confusing, there's no need to worry—we'll go step by step and provide examples on the following pages.

It is important to understand that every valuation technique can be boiled down to one thing: "How much money can I expect to get in return for my initial investment?"

The Discount Cash Flow (DCF) Intrinsic Value Model

Let's start with the "discount cash flow" model. It consists of just six steps. Once you determine what the intrinsic value is, you'll want to compare that value to the market price. The difference between value and price is where you'll see your margin of safety.

Below is an overview of the six steps for the DCF model.

Overview of steps

1) Estimate the free cash flow
2) Estimate the discount factor
3) Calculate the discounted value of free cash flow for ten years
4) Calculate the discounted perpetuity free cash flow (beyond ten years)
5) Calculate the intrinsic value
6) Calculate the intrinsic value per share

Assumptions

- Current free cash flow: $1,000
- The first ten years' annual growth rate of the free cash flow: 6%
- Discount rate: 10%
- Long-term growth rate: 3%
- Shares outstanding: 1,000

Before we go through the first step, I want to highlight that a discount cash flow calculator is provided at BuffettsBooks.com. The calculator goes through the steps you're about to learn. On the website, there is also an instructional video that you can watch to help complement the reading. If you would like to access the calculator and the video, the Web address is:

http://www.buffettsbooks.com/security-analysis/intrinsic-value-calculator-dcf.html

So let's get started with the first step.

1. Estimate the free cash flow

In investing, there is one type of cash flow that is more important than any other. That is cash flow that is *free*. This is the money that can be used solely to benefit the owner, either by distributing the money back through dividends, paying off debt, buying new assets, or even buying back shares. Near the end of Chapter 8 (in the ratio section for the Cash Flow Statement), I go into more depth on how to calculate free cash flow. For now, you can think of free cash flow as the profit that can be paid to the owners without negatively impacting future performance. It's very important that you select a conservative estimate for free cash flow because the entire intrinsic value calculation is based on this number.

For simplicity, let's assume that the base year's, or current year's free cash flow is $1,000. Let's also assume it will grow steadily by 6% annually for the next 10 years. If that were the case, during the future years, the free cash flow would look like this:

Year	1	2	3	4	5	6	7	8	9	10
FCF	$(1+.10)^1$	$(1+.10)^2$	$(1+.10)^3$	$(1+.10)^4$	$(1+.10)^5$	$(1+.10)^6$	$(1+.10)^7$	$(1+.10)^8$	$(1+.10)^9$	$(1+.10)^{10}$
FCF	$1060	$1124	$1191	$1262	$1338	$1419	$1504	$1594	$1689	$1791
GF	6%									

The formula for determining the free cash flow for any given year into the future is the following:

$$FCF_n = BYFCF*(1+GR)^n$$

FCF$_n$ = Free cash flow for year n
BYFCF = Base year free cash flow (current free cash flow)
n = the number of years into the future
GR = the company's estimated annual growth rate

As you think about what percent you should use for the annual growth rate (GR), it's important to consider qualitative and quantitative factors. Your input for this number will drastically impact the intrinsic value so choose wisely and conservatively. A great starting point for picking a percent would be an assessment of the company's historical free cash flow growth rate. That can be found during your assessment of the company's previous cash flow statements.

As you might expect, using past performance is only helpful if the company demonstrates stable and predictable patterns. Another starting point could be the company's average return on equity (ROE) over the past five years. Again, this is reliant on predictable past patterns of performance. If using the ROE, ensure that its trend is either flat or increasing. If a company's ROE has consistently decreased over the past years, it's probably a risky approach to use the average to estimate future performance. As discussed in earlier sections, looking at past results will only take your assessment so far. If you remember, the current value of the company is reliant on the company's ability to earn dollars into the future. After spending time analyzing the company's past performance, I would recommend taking a close look at what the company has planned for the future.

Analysis of future performance will lead to an objective assessment that involves qualitative features; for example, study the company's research and development efforts and get a feel for their future products. More importantly, look hard at the company's current products or services and determine how they might perform as competition increases and time marches on. If you feel like the company's current product line is going to be obsolete in five years, you'll probably want to avoid using past performance indicators for estimating future cash flow growth. Although future earnings projections are rarely accurate, it might help to look at the trends that analysts predict; for example, if you're assessing that a company's free cash flow will increase by 6% over the next ten years, but analysts are showing that the earnings will decrease by 10% next year, there's probably a major disconnect between your assessment and reality.

As you can see, this number is very important. It's ultimately based on the company's ability to earn even more into the future. If you use an extra high growth rate, then your optimism for profits maybe blinding your need for safety. Be accurate, be balanced, and be careful (the ABCs) when selecting a future growth rate.

2. Estimate the discount factor

The discount factor is very similar to the discount rate. The only difference is the discount factor is applied to a specific point in time. Although the two terms sound very similar, their application is not. Be sure you understand that the discount rate is simply one number—a number you select based on risk. The discount factor is numerous numbers depending on what year in the future you're talking about—it is calculated after you select a discount rate. Let's get our hands dirty so the application makes sense. The formula for the discount factor is:

$$DF_n = (1 + DR)^n$$

> DF_n = The discount factor during year n
>
> DR = Discount rate
>
> n = Year being discounted

As you saw previously, the discount rate is an extremely important concept to understand. In essence, the discount rate represents the return you would like to receive for owning the company. If the company is very risky, for example, you might want at least a 20% annual return—therefore your discount rate would be 20%.

A great way to think about the selection of a discount rate is to put yourself into the shoes of the bank lender. Let's say you have a new business that's looking to borrow money. Since the company might have a lot of unknown risks, you require a higher yield on the money you lend. It's also important to consider what kind of return you could get from other opportunities. For example, if you could get a 7% return on a federally issued bond, you should never accept a lower return than that. Therefore, you may want to use a discount rate that's at least double the return of the zero risk federal bond—i.e., 14%. This isn't something that I can provide. It's purely based on your willingness to assume risk. The lower the discount rate you select, the more risk you assume; for example, if you select a discount rate of 5%, that means the intrinsic value will be based on an annual return of 5%. Be careful and leave yourself a margin of safety. If you're new to this process, you'll probably want to always start with a discount rate of higher than 10% until you develop a firm understanding of the process and the risks involved.

Now, to demonstrate the calculation of a discount factor, we'll start by selecting a discount rate of 10%—which represents marginal risk. As a result, our discount factor for the first year would be the following:

$$DF_n = (1+DR)^n$$

$$DF_1 = (1+.10)^1$$

$$DF_1 = 1.10$$

Now, if we were to do this calculation for each future year, you would find that the DF becomes larger and larger; for example, here is the DF for the second future year.

$$DF_n = (1+DR)^n$$

$$DF_2 = (1+.10)^2$$

$$DF_2 = 1.21$$

Using this approach, let's determine the DF for all ten future years.

Year	1	2	3	4	5	6	7	8	9	10
DR	10%	10%	10%	10%	10%	10%	10%	10%	10%	10%
DF	$(1+.10)^1$	$(1+.10)^2$	$(1+.10)^3$	$(1+.10)^4$	$(1+.10)^5$	$(1+.10)^6$	$(1+.10)^7$	$(1+.10)^8$	$(1+.10)^9$	$(1+.10)^{10}$
DF	1.10	1.21	1.33	1.46	1.61	1.77	1.95	2.14	2.36	2.59

That completes this step. Make sure you don't move forward until you're comfortable with the math behind the chart above.

3. Calculate the discounted value of free cash flow for ten years

Now that we have our estimated cash flows and a corresponding discount factor, we can combine them into a discounted free cash flow chart.

Year	1	2	3	4	5	6	7	8	9	10
FCF	$1060	$1124	$1191	$1262	$1338	$1419	$1504	$1594	$1689	$1791
DF	1.10	1.21	1.33	1.46	1.61	1.77	1.95	2.14	2.36	2.59
DFCF	$964	$929	$895	$862	$831	$801	$772	$743	$716	$690
									Sum of DFCF	$8203

The simple formula for arriving at the discounted free cash flow for each year is:

$$DFCF_n = \frac{FCF_n}{DF_n}$$

$DFCF_n$ = Discounted free cash flow for year n
FCF_n = Free cash flow for year n
DF_n = Discount factor for year n

When you look at the numbers above, the discounted FCF number is determined by dividing the free cash flow by the discount factor. Once each year's discounted FCF is determined, all the years are summed together.

Therefore, the sum of all the DFCF values for ten years is $8,203.

Although it might feel like we are complete with our calculation, we're only about half way there. If you remember Buffett's quote about intrinsic value, it calls for the discounted value of all future cash flows. So far we've only done the first ten years. The next step solves that problem.

4. Calculate the discounted perpetuity free cash flow (beyond ten years)

When you are buying a company, you are not only entitled to receive the cash flow over the next ten years; you own the rights to receive cash flows *for as long as it exists.*

For this reason, we also need to include the company's *perpetual* value. To do this, we must look at the cash flows in the years beyond the tenth year. Remember, we have already calculated the discounted value of FCF for the first ten years in step 3. The formula for perpetual value is the following:

$$DPCF = \frac{BYFCF*(1+GR)^{11}*(1+LGR)}{DR-LGR} * \frac{1}{(1+DR)^{11}}$$

DPCF = Discounted perpetuity cash flow
BYFCF = Base year free cash flow
GR = Growth rate of the free cash flow
DR = Discount rate
LGR = Long-term growth rate

Based on the numbers we have used so far, the listed variables have the following values:

DPCF = We are solving for this
BYFCF = $1,000
GR = 6%
DR = 10%
LGR = ?

As you can see, there's a new variable that needs to be determined—the long-term growth rate. Now, this number is nearly impossible to predict. For anyone who thinks they'll be able to predict a company's ability to grow their profits beyond the ten-year mark, best of luck. Although we might feel uncomfortable making those kinds of predictions, we can, however, make a general assumption by asking a simple question:

Is this company going to have the capacity to remain relevant beyond ten years?

For example, do you think a company like Coca-Cola will continue to exist and sustain their market share beyond the ten-year mark? If the answer is yes, then my recommendation is to use a long-term growth rate between 2 or 3 percent. Although we might have a lot of confidence that Coca-Cola would continue to be a profitable business well into the future, simply using the rate of inflation (2-3%) protects your estimate from being too optimistic. Again, this is a technique. You have the capacity to use any rate you would like, but just be prepared for the risk you assume by being too optimistic in your forecasts.

Based on those factors, let's determine the cash flows beyond the ten-year mark. Below is the calculation with the numbers we substituted for the variables (remember we are using 0.03 = LGR for the long-term growth rate):

$$\text{DPCF} = \frac{\$1000*(1+0.06)^{11}*(1+0.03)}{0.10-0.03} * \frac{1}{(1+0.10)^{11}}$$

DPCF = $9,790

Now, depending on your background in math, that calculation might be a little tricky. If that's the case, I highly recommend you use the online calculator at BuffettsBooks.com or Microsoft Excel to conduct the calculation. If you were to select any cell in Microsoft Excel, you could type the following and press enter to get the right answer:

=((1000*(1+0.06)^11*(1+0.03))/(0.10-0.03)*1/(1+0.10)^11)

Now that we have the discounted perpetuity free cash flow, we're almost done! Let's combine our cash flows.

5. Calculate the Intrinsic value

As you might suspect, in order to calculate the intrinsic value (for the entire company), we need to add the first ten years of discounted free cash flows to the perpetuity discounted free cash flows.

Intrinsic value = Sum of DFCF for ten years + DPCF

Intrinsic value = $8,203 + $9,790

Intrinsic value = $17,993

Now, it's very important to recognize that the free cash flow (which is the number that started this calculation) is reported for the entire company; therefore, $17,993 might be in millions or billions of dollars. You can find out how many digits have been rounded by looking at the cash flow statement. It is here that you'll see a note that typically says, "Values in Millions." This means that the intrinsic value of the entire company would be $17,993,000,000. That's a big number that doesn't make sense to a lot of people, so let's fix that in the final step.

6. Calculate the Intrinsic value per share

In order to determine the intrinsic value per share, you'll need to reference the balance sheet or Income statement to see how many common shares are outstanding in the company. This is typically reported at the bottom of the balance sheet in a column labeled, Common *Share Outstanding* or *Ordinary Shares Outstanding.* While looking at the bottom of the balance sheet, be sure to look for the note that specifies if the numbers are reported in millions again. If so, you've got a simple math problem because you can simply divide your intrinsic value from step 5 by the number of common shares outstanding. Let's assume, for example, we found company XYZ has 1,000 shares outstanding:

Intrinsic value per share = Intrinsic value / Common shares outstanding

Intrinsic value per share = $17,993 / 1,000

Intrinsic value per share = $17.99

It's very important to note how many zeros have been rounded off the free cash flow and shares outstanding. If the numbers were rounded differently (i.e., one was millions and the other was billions), you'll need to write out the full amount of digits in the final steps before you conduct your division. It is very uncommon that the numbers would be rounded differently.

So, here's the big question: what the heck does $17.99 mean? Well, it means this: if you could buy one share of company XYZ at $17.99 you could expect a 10% annual return. As you remember, 10% was our discount rate. If you would have selected a higher discount rate, like 20%, you would find that your intrinsic value would be lower. The reason is because you would need to buy company XYZ at an even better price to get the higher return. As you can see, the intrinsic value is completely dependent on the return you seek. This is a concept that very few people actually understand. When someone tells me that they think a particular company has an intrinsic value of, let's say, $100, I quickly respond, "At what discount rate?" Talking about an intrinsic value without a discount rate is like talking about the yin without the yang.

Let's wrap this up and put it into a practical example. Let's say you just calculated the intrinsic value for XYZ at $17.99 with a 10% discount rate. At the same time, let's say company XYZ is trading on the stock market for $25.04. What does that mean?

Simply put, you'll need a lower discount rate for the intrinsic value to match the current trading price of $25.04. If you haven't noticed yet, the intrinsic value and discount rate are inversely proportional. That means when one goes up, the other goes down; therefore, if company XYZ is trading for $25.04, you will need to use a discount rate of lower than 10%. How much lower? Well, that's a very tricky math problem. Luckily for you, I've made an online calculator that automatically calculates the corresponding discount rate for the price the company is trading for on the stock exchange. For this particular example, a market price of $25.04 will create a discount rate of 8.14%—therefore, you can see that the higher market price decreases your annual expected return. Now for the important question: are you still willing to purchase this company even though the higher market price creates a return of 8.14%? Only you can answer that question. Since this is a generic example, underlying risks for owning company XYZ aren't considered. If they were, you would need to qualitatively compare those risks to the yield you expect to receive (8.14%).

The BuffettsBooks Intrinsic Value Model

The more familiar you become with valuing stocks, the quicker you'll realize that everyone has their own take on the process. Through the years, I have really tried to focus on the hints and clues that Warren Buffett has provided through his shareholder letters and countless interviews. It is through those resources that I've found him repeatedly referencing the similarities between the valuation of bonds and stocks. For the next model, you'll find that its core mathematics is based on a bond valuation formula that has been converted into a discount cash flow model for stocks. The specifics of the calculation can be found in the Appendix of this book. Since the math for this valuation technique can be a little cumbersome, I've tried to keep the description of the process simple in this portion of the book. Additionally, you can find this calculator on the BuffettsBooks.com website along with a video tutorial.

Before using this calculator, I want to strongly emphasize the importance of finding stable and predictable companies (Principle 3). Like the discount cash flow model, without using a company that generally has predictable earnings and actions, you'll find the calculator becomes less useful. A company like Exxon-Mobil, for example, has much more predictable earnings than a newly minted public company like Twitter. This doesn't mean that Exxon-Mobil will produce more earnings in the future; it simply means Exxon-Mobil would be easier to value because it's a relatively stable business. This minimizes our exposure to risk in the price we pay for owning the company.

The formula is very simple and only consists of four components. You should have a thorough understanding of each of the components before you start the analysis.

- Book value (Principle 3, Rule 1)
- Dividends (Principle 3, Rule 1)
- Average percent change in book value per year (Principle 3, Rule 1)
- Discount rate (Principle 4, Rule 3)

The BuffettsBooks Intrinsic Value Calculator is similar to the DCF model presented earlier. It also generates an intrinsic value per share (with a corresponding discount rate). In other ways, it is different; for example, the variables for assessing the future cash flows are found through a different process. Instead, you'll be looking at how much money is expected to actually flow back to the owner in terms of dividends and book value growth.

The picture below is a screen-shot of the calculator's inputs at BuffettsBooks.com. We will discuss each of the inputs in detail. The full Web address for accessing the calculator and instructional video is:

http://www.buffettsbooks.com/intelligent-investor/stocks/intrinsic-value-calculator.html

Current Book Value ($):

Old Book Value (S):

# of Years between Book Values:

Calculate

Average Book Value change (%):

"As our definition suggests, intrinsic value is an estimate rather than a precise figure, and it is additionally an estimate that must be changed if interest rates move or forecasts of future cash flows are revised. Two people looking at the same set of facts, moreover - and this would apply even to Charlie and me - will almost inevitably come up with at least slightly different intrinsic value figures. That is one reason we never give you our estimates of intrinsic value." - Warren Buffett

Cash Taken out of business (S):
* This is dividends recieved for 1 year

Current Book Value ($):
*We need to know this so we can determine the base value that's changing

Average Percent Change in book value per year (%):
*This will determine the estimate BV at the end of the next 10 years

Years:
*This will most likely be 10 (if you're comparing a 10 year federal note)

(Discount Rate) 10 year federal note (%):
* Look up the ten year treasury note by clicking on this text

Calculate

Intrinsic Value: $

To make simple use of this calculator, I have divided the approach into seven easy steps. Once you have tried out the steps a couple of times, you will be able to do the calculation quickly. The financial inputs required for using the calculator are all disclosed to the public in a company's annual report and should be easy to find on free Internet sites such as MSN Money, Yahoo Finance, Morningstar, or the company's own website.

Overview of the seven steps for using the calculator

1) Insert book values and find the average book value growth rate
2) Insert cash taken out of the business (or dividend)
3) Insert the current book value
4) Input the average percent change in book value per year (from step 1)
5) Determine the number of years
6) Determine the discount rate
7) Push the calculate button

Assumptions

- Current book value: $30
- Old book value: $10
- Number of years between the two book value figures: 10
- Yearly dividend: $1
- Discount rate: 2.5%

Now, enough talk. Let's get down to business and use the calculator with an example!

1) Insert book values and find the average book value growth rate:

Current Book Value ($): 30

Old Book Value (S): 10

# of Years between Book Values: 10

Calculate

Average Book Value change (%): 11.61

As you may recall, the change in book value over time provides clues into the change in intrinsic value. That is what we are trying to determine in this step. Our starting point is what we call "current book value," and in this generic example I have used $30. We would then go back ten years and look for the "old book value," which in this example is $10. Our calculator generates the average annual output, which is 11.6 %. If you are having problems finding these terms for real companies, I strongly suggest that you watch the video on the calculator's Web page so you can see examples of where to find these variables.

So what does 11.61% mean? It means that in the previous ten years, the shareholders have seen their book value grow, on average, by 11.6% every year. This is equity growth that is ultimately reflected in the company's asset growth or liability reduction. This could be anything, like new equipment for production, or an increased cash account, or a reduction of outstanding debt. Since book value is the owner's claim of the business, the shareholders have become 11.6% wealthier each year from that reinvested capital. As we move forward, this number is going to help us estimate how much the company's equity will grow in the future. It's very important to recognize this historical growth rate as a trend. It doesn't definitively suggest that future growth rates will be the same. Instead, it should be used as a rule of thumb and a starting point for estimating future equity growth rates. Before using this number as an estimate for future growth, be sure you thoroughly understand the future path of the company and its products or services.

2) Insert cash taken out of business

Cash Taken out of business (S):
* This is dividends recieved for 1 year

Current Book Value ($):
*We need to know this so we can determine the base value that's changing

Average Percent Change in book value per year (%):
*This will determine the estimate BV at the end of the next 10 years

Years:
*This will most likely be 10 (if you're comparing a 10 year federal note)

(Discount Rate) 10 year federal note (%):
* Look up the ten year treasury note by clicking on this text

Calculate

Intrinsic Value: $

In the previous step, we were looking backwards in order to get an idea of future performance. The calculator's remaining inputs are all about future cash flows. For the first input, we are going to estimate the average dividend payment you will receive in the next ten years—which can be a challenging task. If our chosen stock follows the first three principles, however, we will likely see a stable or even increasing dividend payment. Look at the trend for dividend payments; as long as it is not declining, you might want to use the current dividend payment as the estimate for the average annual dividend over the next ten years. While this is often a conservative estimate, you can feel comfort in knowing you have a built-in margin of safety if the dividend does increase.

Remember to use the yearly dividend payment, and not the yield. The yearly dividend payment is the actual payment in dollars, while the yield is a floating key ratio that compares the dividend rate to the market price. In this example, I have used $1. That means that over the next ten years, I estimate that $1 per share will be taken out of the business each year and paid to the shareholders as a cash dividend.

3) Insert the current book value

Cash Taken out of business (S):   1
* This is dividends recieved for 1 year

Current Book Value ($):   30
*We need to know this so we can determine the base value that's changing

Average Percent Change in book value per year (%):
*This will determine the estimate BV at the end of the next 10 years

Years:
*This will most likely be 10 (if you're comparing a 10 year federal note)

(Discount Rate) 10 year federal note (%):
* Look up the ten year treasury note by clicking on this text

Calculate

Intrinsic Value: $

As you may recall, we already made an assumption for this in step 1. The current book value is the owner's claim of the company's assets for one share right now.

4) Input the average percent change in book value per year

Cash Taken out of business (S):
* This is dividends recieved for 1 year

> 1

Current Book Value ($):
*We need to know this so we can determine the base value that's changing

> 30

Average Percent Change in book value per year (%):
*This will determine the estimate BV at the end of the next 10 years

> 11.6

Years:
*This will most likely be 10 (if you're comparing a 10 year federal note)

(Discount Rate) 10 year federal note (%):
* Look up the ten year treasury note by clicking on this text

Calculate

Intrinsic Value: $

This is by far the toughest step in the calculation. In any valuation model, one has to make an estimate as to what the future will bring. Warren Buffett has said that even his longtime business partner Charlie Munger and he will come up with different growth rates when evaluating a stock pick. So what should you do?

If the company is stable, a good starting point might be the growth rate you determined in the first step. If you think the company's earnings potential is decelerating, you'll probably want to use a more conservative number. The important thing is that you feel you are using the most accurate estimate for the future. For simplicity, I have used the figure of 11.6% that was found in step 1 in this example. Remember, step 1 is a guide for determining the book value growth rate. It is there for you to assess and determine whether you think the company will continue to grow at that previous rate. This is where qualitative estimates and opinions need to be merged with quantitative analysis.

5) Determine the number of years

Cash Taken out of business (S):   1
* This is dividends recieved for 1 year

Current Book Value ($):   30
*We need to know this so we can determine the base value that's changing

Average Percent Change in book value per year (%):   11.6
*This will determine the estimate BV at the end of the next 10 years

Years: 10
*This will most likely be 10 (if you're comparing a 10 year federal note)

(Discount Rate) 10 year federal note (%):   2.5
* Look up the ten year treasury note by clicking on this text

Calculate

Intrinsic Value: $

I have used ten years as my finite stopping point to estimate the value of future cash flows. This investment horizon was selected so the stock could be relatively compared to a finite ten-year federal bond. This comparison will be discussed more in the next step.

6) Determine the discount rate

This step is extremely important. In principle 4, rule 4, and also the DCF model, we generally discussed how a discount rate works.

If you don't remember the information from that section or it's a little unclear, I strongly recommend you re-read the section.

When we talk about a discount rate, we're really talking about the return we would like to see for a given stock based on the risk we assume; for example, if we were to input a discount rate of 20%, then the calculator would determine an intrinsic value for the stock that would allow the investor to get a 20% annual return. As one might expect, I would likely input a 20% discount rate if I felt the stock had a lot of risk.

Instead of randomly picking a discount rate based on feel and comfort (i.e., 30% for a lot of risk, and 5% for a little risk... etc.), Warren Buffett takes a different approach. Instead, he created a ruler, or measuring stick. That measuring stick is the 10-year Treasury note. Since Buffett holds the opinion that the 10-year Treasury note is zero risk to the investor, it becomes a baseline; for example, if the 10-year Treasury note is returning 2.5% today, then he knows that should be his minimum acceptable return— therefore, if we use this rate as our discount rate, then we can relatively compare all investments on the same playing field.

Now this is very important! Because you are using 2.5% for your discount rate, this also means that the intrinsic value will price the stock with an annual return of 2.5% per year. Don't forget that! We'll discuss this more after you calculate the intrinsic value. As a side note, you can find daily updates on the 10-year Treasury note at this Web address: http://www.treasury.gov/resource-center/data-chart-center/interest-rates/Pages/TextView.aspx?data=yield. I've provided a quick link to this address: to the right side of the discount rate input box on the calculator, you will find a text that reads "*Look up the ten-year Treasury note by clicking on this text."

7) Push the calculate button!

Cash Taken out of business (S):
* This is dividends recieved for 1 year

| 1 |

Current Book Value ($):
*We need to know this so we can determine the base value that's changing

| 30 |

Average Percent Change in book value per year (%):
*This will determine the estimate BV at the end of the next 10 years

| 11.6 |

Years:
*This will most likely be 10 (if you're comparing a 10 year federal note)

| 10 |

(Discount Rate) 10 year federal note (%):
* Look up the ten year treasury note by clicking on this text

| 2.5 |

Calculate

Intrinsic Value: $

| 78.98 |

Based on the estimates and assumption, we have found that the intrinsic value of the stock is $78.98 at a 2.5% discount rate. Let us make a quick stop and look behind what has happened in the six simple steps.

To arrive at an intrinsic value of $78.98, we have assumed that the stock will pay out a $1 annual dividend over the next ten years. Additionally, we estimated that the company would retain the rest of their earnings and the current book value of $30 will grow by 11.6% each year. Based on those cash flows over the next ten years, we have discounted that money by the risk-free ten-year federal bond.

So what the heck does that mean? Well, based on your inputs, the calculator suggests that if you could buy this stock today for $78.98, you could expect a 2.5% annual return for the next ten years.

To make things more realistic, let's assume that this company is currently trading on the stock market for $90. What does that mean? Assuming all your estimates for future earnings are valid, this means you'll get an even smaller return than 2.5% if you buy the stock at $90.

So your next question is probably "How much smaller than 2.5%?" To determine that with the calculator is relatively simple, but it does require a little trial and error. To figure out the return you can expect based on the company currently trading for $90, simply adjust the discount rate and recalculate until the output (the intrinsic value) reads $90.

I'm sure it didn't take long for you to see that a 1% discount rate roughly gives you $90. So, going back to the ruler analogy with the 10-year Treasury note, we can now draw a comparison. We can assume that if this stock was priced on the stock market for $90, the Treasury note would provide a 2.5 times better return. This was simply determined by looking at the stock return of 1% at its current market price, and comparing it to the Treasury note's return of 2.5%.

Now, let's assume the stock market price was below our initial intrinsic value of $78.98. For simplicity, let's say the stock trades for $60. What's your expected return at that price?

Like before, use the trial and error method to adjust the discount rate to 5.5% and you will get an intrinsic value of $60. Again, let's compare the stock to the Treasury note. Based on a market price of $60, the stock will provide a 2.2 times higher return than the Treasury note.

As you can see, the intrinsic value is always relative to a discount rate.

Finding the margin of safety

As you can see from the previous examples, your margin of safety is based on the margin of return you expect to receive over the 10-year federal note. If you find a stock that meets all four principles and is priced on the market at a 15% annual return, your margin of safety is 6 times higher than a 2.5% Treasury note.

When you look at Buffett's quote on intrinsic value, he states that estimates must be changed if interest rates change. What he refers to is the margin of safety an investor receives; for example, let's say that we have a stock that's priced at $50 and we think that gives us a 7.5% return. Let's also say that the interest rate on a 10-year Treasury note changed from 2.5% to 5% over a year's period. Assuming the stock price didn't change during that period (to make the example simple), we can quickly see how our margin of safety has drastically changed during that time.

When interest rates were 2.5%, our stock provided a return 3 times higher than a zero risk investment.

When interest rates moved to 5.0%, our stock only provided 1.5 times the return of the zero risk investment.

Although our stock didn't change at all, our margin of safety did. This is an extremely important consideration for any investor to understand.

Now, everyone likes to have hard fast rules for making decisions, but this is where valuing stocks becomes an art. Only you know how much risk you're willing to assume for any particular venture.

Regardless of which method we use to assess the stock, the decision is the same. A higher discount, or margin of safety, if you like, will result in a higher return if you can get the investment at the corresponding price. If you are not happy about the discount or the expected return you will receive, you can wait for the stock price to drop. The nice thing about the calculator is you can adjust the numbers to see how far the stock price should drop before it becomes attractive.

Which calculator should I use?

As you obviously saw, you've got two choices for calculating the intrinsic value of a company. The DCF model allowed you to estimate the company's value buy discounting cash flows into perpetuity. The second calculator provided a finite solution and only summed the cash flows for a ten-year period. Additionally, the two calculators used different numbers to represent future cash flows. The DCF Model simply used free cash flow, and the BuffettsBooks calculator used dividends plus book value growth.

Like anything, there are advantages and disadvantages between both choices. When deciding which calculator to use, the best advice is probably to use the one that provides the most conservative estimate. That may change from company to company as you run the numbers through both calculators. Although the BuffettsBooks calculator may be easier to use because it keeps all the numbers in a per share basis, that model comes with limitations:

Limitations with the BuffettsBooks intrinsic calculator

The calculator is a neat tool, but there are typically four situations where it is less useful and where one may choose the DCF model instead.

i) *It only works if a stock fulfills all four of Warren Buffett's principles*

If the company does not follow Warren Buffett's four principles, the calculator will give you invalid results. The calculator is built upon predictability and stability, and if all of the criteria are not met, the output will likewise become unpredictable and unstable. Specifically, you'll want to find companies that have demonstrated the ability to have stable and predictable Returns on Equity (ROE). If a company lacks certain aspects of the principles discussed, those aspects should be assessed as additional risk to the investor. These qualitative aspects should be accounted for by lowering the book value growth rate, lowering the dividend rate, requiring a higher discount rate, or not even evaluating the stock all together.

ii) *High-growth companies*

A key element in the calculator is the compounding of book value. High-growth companies naturally have a better opportunity to grow their book value compared to large, slow-growth companies, even if it's for a limited period of time. These growth rates will yield very high intrinsic values in the calculator. I would recommend not using more than 13-15% for book value growth in the calculator, even if the company has shown much higher growth over the past ten years. For high-growth companies, the DCF

113

model will provide better estimates because you can limit the number of years at a high growth rate.

iii) *High degree of share buy-back*

If the company you're interested in uses share buy-backs to a high degree, you should be very careful using the calculator. Buy-backs distort the book value, which in turn also distorts the intrinsic value. You can determine how many share buy-backs a company is conducting by looking at the cash flow statement. In relative terms, if the buy-backs are generally small, it will have a small impact on your calculation, but if it's corporate strategy to reduce the number of shares outstanding, you'll probably want to use the DCF model instead.

iv) *Stock Splits*

If the company you're interested in valuing has had a history of stock splits, you'll find that the historical book value growth rate isn't representative of its actual performance. As a result, you'll need to account for this disparity when assessing how much the book value may grow in the future. It may be easier to use the DCF model in an effort to avoid this potential error.

As a final note, I want to highlight that the BuffettsBooks forum has a great community of very smart investors who can help explain and clarify any questions you have relating to this subject. In fact, the forum already has a thread of hundreds of questions and answers relating to the calculation of intrinsic value. Feel free to correspond with any of the users at:

http://buffettsbooks.com/money-forum/

Rule 6—The right time to sell

One factor is knowing when to buy a stock. Another, which is just as important, is knowing when to exit. Contrary to when you search for new investment objects, you have a huge advantage when it comes to your decision to sell. You already know the company; therefore you have a good idea of the fair value, and also the company's future path. So should you sell?

Often, people think that they should sell either because a stock has decreased or increased by a certain price. Although that might be an important consideration, that's only one factor of many, in a larger picture.

Unless you really need the money personally, you might want to consider the impacts of capital gains and bank fees before you impulsively switch assets. Looking at your decisions from the most fundamental level, you should revert back to Warren Buffett's four principles:

> Is the company still managed by vigilant leaders?

> Does the company still have products and services that have long-term prospects?

> Are the company's earnings and debt management still stable and predictable?

> Based on the projected cash flows, what kind of return do you expect at the current trading price?

If any one of these rules is being breached, it's probably a smart decision to consider the opportunity costs associated with continuing your ownership versus purchasing a new asset.

Another valid reason for selling a stock would be if you feel that the stock is taking up too much of your portfolio; hence, you want to control your exposure risk. This is really a very sensitive topic for many value investors. As I mentioned earlier in the book, Warren Buffett strongly believes that concentration of your portfolio actually diminishes your risk. He compares this strategy with having Michael Jordan on your team: would you substitute him because he is scoring all the points?

Although Buffett likes a focused portfolio, he still keeps more than ten different picks in his portfolio. In the end, value investors should make this decision and feel comfortable. If you feel that 20% or 35% of your portfolio in one stock is too risky, you should listen to your intuition. Even the best investors make mistakes when picking stocks, and you don't want to be fully invested with only one stock, even if you deem it the very best pick on the entire market.

So let's go back to Buffett's final principle—buying at attractive prices. As you might suspect, you should sell your stock if you can place your money in another, more profitable, investment. It is as simple as that! It is great if you expect your favorite stock to increase by 8% a year, but if you can find another investment that yields 9%, why not pick the winner? Although the decision to switch assets might seem simple and straightforward, one must consider the costs associated with switching assets before making that decision. On BuffettsBooks.com, we have provided a sell calculator and video to help you through the process of accounting for capital gains and growth projections. The calculator can be found at the following Web address:

http://www.buffettsbooks.com/security-analysis/when-to-sell-shares.html

In conjunction with the sell calculator, you'll also need to access one of the intrinsic value calculators to get the yield projections. In order to facilitate your decision and use of the online calculators, an outline is provided below to assist in the thought process and methodology.

To decide if you should keep or sell your current holding (stock A), or invest in another (stock B), follow these four easy steps:

1) Calculate the expected annual return for stocks A and B based on the current market prices

2) Subtract the cost of capital gains tax from stock A

3) Calculate whether stock A or B yields the highest expected annual return based on a given timeframe.

Let's look at each of the steps in detail.

1) Calculate the expected annual return for stocks A and B based on the current market prices

As you will recall, the intrinsic value calculation was adjusted to account for the return you could expect at a given market price. Depending on which intrinsic value model you use, you'll either apply the trial-and-error approach with the BuffettsBooks intrinsic value calculator or you can simply input the current market price (last input) for the DCF calculator. Either way, you need to determine the appropriate discount rate that makes the intrinsic value equal to the current market price. You'll need to do this for both stocks: once for your current holding and once when you evaluate the new pick. Imagine in this example that, after determining that discount rate for each pick, the expected annual return is 6% for stock A and 9% for stock B. If you have difficulty determining these expected annual returns, you can reference the video that's located on the same Web page as the sell calculator.

2) Subtract the cost of capital gains tax from stock A

In Principle 2, Rule 2 we looked at the different capital gains that must be paid if you sell a stock with profit. Let's have a quick review:

2014 Short and Long-term Capital Gains tax for filing as a single person		
Ordinary Income brackets	Short-Term Capital Gains Tax	Long-Term Capital Gains and dividend Tax
$0 to $9,075	10%	0%
$9,076 to $36,900	15%	0%
$36,901 to $89,350	25%	15%
$89,351 to $186,350	28%	15%
$186,351 to $405,100	33%	15%
$405,101 to $406,750	35%	15%
More than $406,750	39.6%	20%

Short-term capital gain < 1 year

Let us say that you have held stock A for less than a year and your annual income tax bracket is $100,000. As a result, your capital gains tax would be 28%. Imagine that you initially purchased stock A for $60 and it has now increased to $100. In this case, you would have to pay $11.20 ($40*28%) in taxes per share and you would have a total of $88.80 ($100-$11.20) left for investing into stock B.

Remember it is only the profit that you are paying capital gains taxes on ($100-$60), not the full amount.

3) **Calculate whether stocks A or B yield the highest expected annual return based on a given timeframe.**

BuffettsBooks Sell Calculator

What is price of the stock you currently own?	$100.00
How many shares of this stock do you own?	1
What annual discount rate makes the intrinsic value equal to the market price for the stock you currently own? You can watch a method for determining this input at the 19.58 minute mark in the video above.	9%
What will be the capital gains tax rate if you decide to sell your current stock?	28%
What gains have you made while owning your current stock pick?	$40
For the new stock pick, what annual discount rate makes the intrinsic value equal to the market price? You can watch a method for determining this input at the 26.24 minute mark in the video above.	10%

(Show sell criteria)

	Current Stock	New Stock
0	$100	$89
5	$154	$143
10	$237	$231
15	$364	$372
20	$560	$599
25	$862	$964
30	$1,327	$1,553

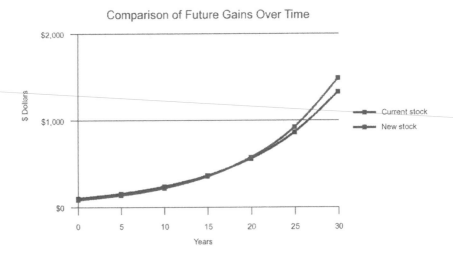

Above, you can see a screen capture for the inputs we have described on the sell calculator at BuffettsBooks.com. Noteworthy highlights are the amount of time it takes (almost 15 years) for the investor to recuperate their capital gains loss when switching assets. Although the investor eventually makes more money by switching into a higher yielding asset, the time associated with that recovery is the part that needs to be considered. This is the whole purpose of using the sell calculator—to determine how long will it take an investor to recover the principal that was lost due to frictional costs (i.e., taxes). As you change the variables in the calculator, you'll quickly find that the inputs for capital gains and growth rates will drastically change the timeframe for recovering tax expenses.

Summing up: Buy at attractive prices

1) Margin of safety is the difference between the intrinsic value and the current share price. You want as much margin as possible to minimize risk.

2) A price/earnings ratio below 15 is a rule of thumb and starting point to finding decently priced stocks. The lower the price/earnings ratio, the less you have to pay for $1 of earnings.

3) A price/book value below 1.5 is a rule of thumb and starting point for reducing your exposure to risk. A key ratio of 1 means that the investor pays $1 of price for every $1 of equity in the company. If a company has a high price/book ratio, you can minimize your risk if the company has a very large moat (i.e., a valuable brand and/or patent).

4) A treasury bond can be used as a ruler, or benchmark, for quantifying the value of stocks. Specifically, it can be used as a discount rate so stocks can be priced in a manner that's compared to a zero risk investment. By making this comparison, you'll protect yourself in a high-interest environment, because stocks will become less attractive, whereas in a low-interest environment stocks become more valuable. Buffett uses the 10-year federal note as a starting point.

5) The discount cash flow (DCF) calculator is a model that calculates a company's intrinsic value. This model uses the free cash flow of a company and sums its expected growth into eternity (or perpetuity). All those cash flows are then discounted back to today's value in order to determine a corresponding intrinsic value.

6) The BuffettsBooks Intrinsic Value Calculator is similar to the DCF model but it sums cash flows into a finite period (i.e., ten years). Additionally, the BuffettsBooks calculator uses per share numbers to estimate cash flow from dividends and book value growth. To apply the model, a stock must fulfill all four principles.

7) A stock should be sold if the company is breaking one or more of Warren Buffett's principles, if it takes up too much of your portfolio, or if you can get a better return from another investment.

Half-time roll-up

That was the first half of the book. By now you know the fundamentals that Warren Buffett uses to evaluate stocks. You know how to look at the stock market and why you should be happy when the stock market is dropping. You have been introduced to concepts that every stock investor should be aware of about interest rates, inflation and bonds; you have also been introduced to the three main financial statements. During the next half of this book, we are going to get into the details of accounting. If things have moved too fast up to this point, you might want to reread previous section, or watch some of the free video lessons at our website to help clarify any questions or ambiguity.

Chapter 5

Financial Statements and the Stock Investor

"Accounting is the language of business."—Warren Buffett

Just as you should learn the local language if you want to integrate into a foreign country, you will be lost in value investing if you cannot read financial statements.

In Chapter 3, I briefly introduced the three main financial statements. The purpose was to provide you with a basic understanding of accounting so you could identify and apply Warren Buffett's four principles. In this chapter, I will not only give you an insight into why accounting is relevant, but I will deep-dive into the composition of each line in the three financial statements.

Let's get started...

Why are financial statements important to the stock investor?

You are probably well aware that investors eagerly wait for the company's annual and quarterly reports in order to gauge the value of their investments. As you've already started to learn, the value of a business is entirely dependent on how these numbers move and are expected to move into the future. But before we go further down the path of detailed accounting, there are a few items that need to be presented.

Imagine that the Disney Company had 1,000 shares outstanding. If that were the case, potentially there could be 1,000 company owners. Understanding this fundamental concept, we can now introduce the idea of a board of directors (BOD). Since most businesses are divided into much more than 1,000 shares, the number of owners is typically in the thousands or millions. With so many people owning a share of the business, a BOD is a governing body that represents the voice of all those owners.

This is often referred to as the principal-agent discussion, and if that rings a bell it is because I previously introduced this in Chapter 4. The agent-principle relationship is probably the major reason financial statements are so important. Investors can analyze the information presented in the annual accounts and investigate the inner workings of the organization. The annual accounts are the most important form of communication between the BOD and the shareholders. As this information is distributed to all the shareholders, thousands of eyes should theoretically be reviewing the authenticity of the company's performance.

Generally, you will find that most publically traded businesses have an "Investor Relations" section in their website. Here you should find the recent reports, dividend history, video/audio conference calls about the previous quarter's report. The more information you find in this investor relations area, the better. As an investor, I always like to see a thorough investor relation's hub for information. Without a firm understanding of the language of business, or accounting, the message being conveyed to all the owners will be missed.

Accounting basics at a glance

Now let's look at the very basics of accounting. By the time you study the annual report, a lot of work has already been done by the accountants. Every accountant knows the world of debits and credits, but as an investor you might not understand the "plumbing" of how all the money moves between each of the financial statements and subsequent accounts.

Chapter 5 Financial Statements and the Stock Investor

The world of debits and credits

"Every debit must have a credit." This mantra forms the basis of all accounting concepts and standards developed to date. The system of debits and credits is known as the double-entry system. As the name implies, every entry has a dual impact on the financial accounts. To take a simple example, when a person buys a product, what is the impact of that action? The purchase results in an outflow of cash while the inflow is in the form of a product or service.

Now let's apply this principle to a corporation. When a company purchases raw materials with cash from its corporate bank account, the outflow would be in the form of cash, whereas the inflow is in the form of raw materials to make their products. Dual impact once again.

A company organizes all their financial data into records called accounts. This organization is referred to as the "chart of accounts." If a business is very large and has many moving divisions, the chart of accounts can become extremely large and cumbersome. Luckily for us, all these accounts are outlined and summarized in the income statement and balance sheet. So if you crack open those two financial statements, they provide the foundation for all the different accounts a business might have. As you probably recall from Chapter 3, I introduced the following:

The Income Statement:

    Revenues
    Expenses

The Balance Sheet:

    Assets
    Liabilities
    Equity

Now, as we move forward and briefly discuss a few examples of how double-entry accounting works, please don't get discouraged. There's no way a person seeing this for the first time is going to holistically understand all the terminology and application. The reason it's being explained is to provide you with a general understanding of the financial statements and what has happened before you read them.

If you have had a brief encounter with accounting before, you might benefit from the chart below. This chart characterizes the proper terminology for whether an account is being debited or credited. For example, if a revenue is added to the income statement, that's referred to as a credit.

The Income Statement:	Debit	Credit
Revenues (or Income)	Decrease	Increase
Expenses	Increase	Decrease

The Balance Sheet:	Debit	Credit
Assets	Increase	Decrease
Liabilities	Decrease	Increase
Owner's Equity	Decrease	Increase

Let's start with a T-account. A T-account is nothing more than a "T" diagram with debits listed on the left and credits listed on the right. This is important: debits are always on the left and credits are always on the right. This is what a T-account looks like:

Cash

(Asset row on the Balance sheet)

Debit	Credit

Looks simple enough, doesn't it? So let's try it out with an example. Let's say a company wants to borrow $10,000 from the bank on January 1st. As a result of the loan, the company's cash on hand increases by $10,000. Before we simply add that into the T-account, we must also consider the doubly entry. It is not enough that we just make a journal entry of $10,000 to our company. Someone obviously wants the money back if we have borrowed it, and that must be reflected in the double-entry.

In this case, we would call that account the *notes payable* and increase it by $10,000. Notes payable is a fancy accounting term that means "loans that need to be paid." So if we were going to mark this double-entry into our T-accounts, it would look something like this:

Cash

(Asset row on the Balance sheet)

Debit	Credit
(Increases any Asset Account)	(Decreases any Asset Account)
Today $10,000	

Notes Payable

(Liability row on the Balance sheet)

Debit	Credit
(Decreases any Liability Account)	(Increases any Liability Account)
	$10,000 Today

Try to stop for a moment and think about the mechanics behind what just happened. We now own $10,000 that we did not have before. Types of assets could be buildings, cars, or, as in this situation, cash. To increase our cash holding, we therefore debit the asset column.

On the other hand, it is money that we have borrowed from a bank. So before we can go out and spend it, we also want our accounts to reflect what we need to pay back. We therefore credit a similar amount of $10,000, increasing the liabilities column under Notes Payable.

Hopefully, this seems fairly easy and straightforward. Let's try a follow-on example. Let's assume that we move forward six days and we now want to make a payment on our outstanding loan—or Notes Payable account. Let's say we take $1,000 in cash and make a payment on the loan. What would our T-account look like then?

Cash
(Asset row on the Balance sheet)

Debit	Credit
(Increases any Asset Account)	(Decreases any Asset Account)
1 JAN Entry $10,000	$1,000 Entry 7 JAN
7 JAN Balance $9,000	

Notes Payable
(Liability row on the Balance sheet)

Debit	Credit
(Decreases any Liability Account)	(Increases any Liability Account)
7 JAN Entry $1,000	$1,000 Entry 7 JAN
	$9,000 Balance 7 JAN

The idea behind this is actually quite simple. We would now only have $9,000 in cash, but on the contrary we would only have borrowed a total of $9,000 from the bank. You probably see now why this is called double-entry accounting.

Although double-entry accounting can get quite complex, don't be worried. Your head should not be spinning about the terminology of debits and credits on T accounts. As a successful stock market investor, your job is to focus on the big picture. Although double-entry accounting is the foundation for financial statements, you'll probably never have to see another T-account diagram ever again. The important point is this: If money listed on a financial statement gets bigger or smaller from one reporting period to the next, we know the money went somewhere!

The investigation into where the money went is the part that makes you a smart and successful investor. This investigation is the goal for the rest of the book; for example, you might see a company's cash account really grow from one year to the next. An amateur investor would simply stop there and say that's a great thing.

The serious stock investor, however, will go straight to the cash flow statement and see where the cash came from. If the cash came from a loan, is that something to get excited about? Of course not! What if the cash came from the net income? Well if that's the case, that's a great thing for the stock investor. Tracking how the money flows through a business is like watching a plumber determine where the leak is in a house. He starts at the source, where the water enters the main valve into the house (the net income), and he ends at the sink (the growing/decreasing equity and/ or dividend). A well-managed and profitable business will show a strong flow of cash through the plumbing of the accounts.

Cash-based accounting

The first accounting regime you should know about is cash-based accounting, and the second is accrual accounting. As an intelligent stock investor, you'll definitely want to become familiar with the latter—accrual accounting. Since publically traded companies are forced to use accrual accounting, that is what we'll primarily be discussing throughout the remainder of the book.

Before moving to accrual accounting, let's start with the easy concepts first. Cash-based accounting is essentially what the name says: accounting based on cash. A transaction is recorded only when cash is physically or digitally received into the bank account. It sounds easy enough, doesn't it? It really is. Most people live their lives on a cash basis, so the subject should be familiar; for example, if you buy a cup of coffee at a Starbucks, you receive your coffee right after the cash leaves your pocket. This is cash-based accounting.

Now, very often in business the transfer of goods and services will not happen simultaneously with the cash payment. Consider a company working on a project that gets completed before the year's end. Payment for the project, however, is received at the beginning of the following year. If the company is following cash- based accounting, the transaction would be recorded in the second year because the cash didn't arrive in the account until then. This is the fundamental principle underlying cash-based accounting: transactions are recorded on the basis of inflow or outflow of cash when the money actually changes accounts, not when the service or product is provided or received.

This form of accounting is useful for small businesses that operate on a cash basis. Although this might be alright for "mom and pop"-style businesses, accounting laws do not allow for larger companies to conduct cash-based accounting. The reason for this is because it represents a slow and delayed way of tracking revenues and expenses. This is where *accrual accounting* comes in.

Accrual accounting

Accrual accounting simply states that expenditures must be recorded when incurred and not when paid. Similarly, revenue must be recorded when there is an outflow of services or goods, not when the payment is realized. Let's make this really simple to understand. Let's say you're trying to start a new business and your product is the world's best beach ball. In order to get your product into as many stores as possible, you provide a sample to Wal-Mart.

After Wal-Mart looks at your beach ball, they decide to give you a purchase order of 10,000 units. Part of the deal on the purchase order is that payment will be made in *NET 90 days*. This means that, after you provide the product, Wal-Mart has 90 days to pay you for all those beach balls. According to accrual accounting, even though you won't receive money from Wal-Mart for 90 days, you would still list this sale on the financial books today.

The important part to understand at this point is that the payment hasn't occurred yet. In fact, the payment won't be made for another 90 days.

When you are analyzing financial statements, namely the income statement and balance sheet, always remember that the publicly traded companies are based on accrual accounting. As a result, you will have a more current and candid picture of the company's performance. Now, with every positive comes a negative: although accrual accounting provides a higher level of fidelity and timeliness, many critics say it fails to show the actual cash flow.

Let's go back to the Wal-Mart example. Although we have listed the sale in our financial statements, there is nothing preventing Wal-Mart from potentially defaulting on the payment. Now, Wal-Mart is probably a bad example for this scenario, but the idea of a payment not being made is very important and applicable in some cases. Like people, many businesses can go bankrupt. If this is the case, the numbers being reported may not actually materialize into the account.

Before you get scared and look at accrual accounting as a corrupt way of doing business, let me reintroduce the purpose of the cash flow statement—which was first described in Chapter 3. So far, we've only talked about the income statement and balance sheet, but as you'll see, the cash flow statement helps add clarity to the fog of accrual accounting.

Prior to 1987, companies only reported their financial information on the income statement and balance sheet. Unfortunately for investors, this made it very difficult to determine certain things; for example, on a balance sheet, investors could see that a company might have increased the size of their buildings or equipment, but where did the money come from that paid for this? Also, if you looked at the bottom line of the income statement, an investor would see the net income. This is nice to know, but how much of that income was actually turned into cash for the business to use? In order to fix this problem and provide owners and investors a more comprehensive look at the businesses accounting, it was decided that companies should adopt cash flow statements in their reporting.

A short recap

Here's a recap for those feeling overwhelmed. The accounting system is based on double entries. For every debit, there must be a credit. Each entry within the accounting system has a dual impact, making it possible to balance... a balance sheet. The debits and credits might be based on cash inflows and outflows or on product and service inflows and outflows. The cash-based accounting system is subject to much criticism, and in order to provide a true and fair view, standards require that publicly traded companies incorporate the accrual accounting system. Although accrual accounting might count funds that haven't actually been paid, it provides a clearer and realistic picture of the company's performance—especially for stock investors. A great way to account for any inconsistencies caused from accrual accounting is by thoroughly understanding the cash flow statement.

Chapter 6
Income Statement in Detail

Do you remember Warren Buffett's statement about accounting being the language of business? Well, with that in mind, you should consider the following chapters as learning the finer points of grammar in a new language. When you visit a foreign country, you'll do fine with the most common phrases; but if you *really* want to master another language, you need to learn the fine grammar *while* you speak the language. Let's start by diving into the income statement.

Introduction to the income statement

As you have probably already realized, in investing and accounting we have a lot of words for the same thing. This is true for the income statement, which is referred to as the profit and loss statement, the statement of operations, and the statement of income. Regardless of all these names (which I'm convinced are used to confuse people), the income statement's sole purpose is to show a company's profitability over a given period of time.

As I have said many times, financial statements are really easy to understand, and the income statement is no different. Still, one reason so few understand them is because income statements always look different. Yes, that's right! Income statements always seem to have different lines and the names of the accounts can change depending on which company you are looking at; for example, one company might call *revenue, "turnover"* and another company may seem to forget to include *depreciation*, while a competitor has disclosed it as a major expense.

Don't be confused by all of this. All income statements are essentially built the same way. Let me give you an example:

Annual (year 2014) Income statement		in millions
1	Revenue	13,279
2	Cost of revenue	5,348
1-2 = 3	Gross Margin	7,931
4	Sales and Marketing expenses	1,105
5	Research and development expenses	863
6	General and Administration expenses	538
7	Other operating expenses	1,350
4+5+6+7 = 8	Operating expenses	3,856
3-8 = 9	Income from operations	4,075
10	Net interest income/(expenses)	(135)
11	Extraordinary income/(expenses)	275
12	Income taxes	1,352
9+10+11-12 = 13	Net income	2,863

You were introduced to this income statement in Chapter 3. As we move through this chapter, I will break down each line separately to enable a full understanding of the income statement. Let's start learning about this statement by looking at the very top. The first thing you should notice is the term, or duration, of the statement. This particular example says we are looking at an annual statement for 2014. The income statement will typically be an annual or quarterly report. Next, look at the first (1) and last line (13). These two lines are the most important items on the statement. Think of Revenue as all the sales the company makes, and Net Income as the "bottom line" profit those sales produced; for example, Coca-Cola might sell a 2-liter bottle for $2.00 (line 1—Revenue), but the profit for that sale might be $0.20 (line 13—Net Income). Now for the easy part: all the numbers in between the first and last line are the expenses and/or credits that brought the revenue from $2.00 to a profit line of $0.20. In the statement above, you can see that the overall revenue is $13,279. That revenue produced a profit (or net income) of $2,863.

The difference between revenue and gain

So what do the different lines in the income statement mean and how are they important? To answer this question, I'll break it down into steps. First, however, let's look at an outline of the key components of the income statement:

1. Revenues and gains

    a. Revenues generated from primary activities

    b. Revenues generated from secondary activities

    c. Gains.

2. Expenses and losses

    a. Expenses generated from primary activities

    b. Expenses generated from secondary activities

    c. Expenses generated from financial activities

    d. Losses.

As we look at this list, you can see all the items under row 1 involve a positive cash flow, while items under row 2 involve a negative cash flow. The difference between these two rows is the bottom line of the income statement, which is the net income or net loss.

Let's start by discussing the revenues and gains. This is the part every investor should enjoy—the topic of earning money for the company. As we look at the three categories (primary activities, secondary activities and gains), each one adds a different type of positive cash flow to the income statement. Remember, the income statement is cumulative for a specified period of time. If you sold one bottle of your $1 soft drinks every day for three months, your revenues on the quarterly income statement would be $90. Easy enough.

As you might expect, many million- and billion-dollar businesses have numerous ways to make money. Sticking with our example, they might not only sell soda, but they might also receive revenues from other investments or loans they've made. All of this positive revenue is recorded on the income statement, but it's categorized differently. The following are the differences between the three types of revenues/gains:

1.a. Revenues from primary activities: This is probably the easiest type of revenue for new investors to understand. Simply put, it's the revenue received for the sale of the company's primary product or service. Going back to our soft drinks example, all of the revenue logged on the income statement for the sale of soft drinks would be considered revenue from primary activities, or operating revenues. In this example, the company has a primary revenue of $13,279 (line 1).

1.b. Revenues from secondary activities: As I mentioned earlier, not all revenue comes from the sale of a primary product or service; for example, let's say that your soft drinks business has $1,000 cash on hand in a savings account from previous sales. During the three months of selling soft drinks, the $1,000 of cash sitting in an interest-bearing savings account produced revenue of $2.50 from 1% annual interest.

In an effort to properly account for all of the company's revenues, secondary activities are usually included in an income statement under the line titled *net interest income*. It is sometimes referred to as *other income* if it also includes other revenues not made from financial activities. You should not be too focused on what the line is called, but simply be aware that other forms of revenue exist.

In the numbered income statement shown above, we can see that there is a $135 deficit. This means that in the previous year, there have been higher expenses for financial activities than for secondary revenue. We will return to this in section 2.c to explain further.

1.c. Gains: Let's assume that the soft drinks company you own has a really awesome location. When you purchased this location five years ago, you purchased it for $1,000. Although the location is really good, you want to move to a bigger and more spacious building. As a result, you need to sell the old land. When you put the land on the market, you're very excited to find that you're able to sell it for $1,500. That's a $500 gain. From time to time, you'll see gains listed on the income statement as "Gain (Loss) on Sale of Assets." It's very important to understand that gains are not considered operating income. That is also why gains and losses are sometimes referred to as *extraordinary income (expense)*.

For simplicity in our generic income statement, I only use a single line to capture the difference between all extraordinary income and expenses. In this example, it is $275, which is a positive number and therefore a gain.

Annual (year 2014) Income statement			in millions
1	Revenue	13,279	1a) Revenue from primary activities
2	Cost of revenue	5,348	
1-2 = 3	Gross margin	7,931	
4	Sales and marketing expenses	1,105	
5	Research and development expenses	863	
6	General and administration expenses	538	
7	Other operating expenses	1,350	
4+5+6+7 = 8	Operating expenses	3,856	
3-8 = 9	Income from operations	4,075	
10	Net interest income/ (expenses)	(135)	1b) Revenue from secondary activities
11	Extraordinary income/ (expenses)	275	1c) Gains
12	Income taxes	1,352	
9+10+11-12 = 13	Net income	2,863	

So, that's it for the positive numbers being listed on the income statement. Just like the revenues and gains, the negative numbers have very similar categories.

The difference between expenses and losses

2.a. Expenses generated from primary activities: I expect you are already anticipating this, but expenses from primary activities are only those expenses that occur from producing operating revenues; for example, if our primary revenue involves selling soft drinks, our primary expenses would involve buying sugar and tin for the cans. For our company, we have primary expenses of $5,348. This is listed on the income statement as "Cost of Revenue" (line 2).

2.b. Expenses generated from secondary activities: If an expense is made by the business and it doesn't directly relate to the materials or labor used to make the primary product, it's considered an expense generated from secondary activities. You'll often find these expenses listed on the income statement after the primary activity expenses. Secondary activity expenses look like this on the income statement:

> Sales and marketing expenses
> Research and development expenses
> General and administrative expenses
> Other operating expenses

Keep in mind that you will often find other terms for secondary expenses that are not mentioned above. Either way, remember that a company cannot omit reporting expenses. It is simply a question of how the company chooses to disclose it. For instance, take an expense like depreciation on the company's cars. The company can choose to disclose depreciation on a single line, as seen above, or to allocate the depreciation on the specific cars to the departments to which the cars belong. That means that some depreciation expenses will be allocated to Sales and Marketing, while other expenses will be allocated to Research and Development, and so on.

In the example, there are expenses from secondary activities, or operating expenses of $3,856 (line 8).

2.c. Expenses from financial activities: On the face of it, expenses from financial activities may look as if they should be clustered with the expenses from secondary activities. After all, they are expenses originating from borrowed money, and those same loans keep the business running.

Although that might make intuitive sense, we disclose this separately as *interest expenses*, as they are not part of the daily business. This is made clearer when we look at line number 10, which is presented away from the operations. In the case of our example company, it's expenses from financial activities of $135. Since this account is combined with the secondary revenues, which were discussed in section 1.b., we now see that the company owed more interest to banks or lenders than the company received in interest payments from bonds or other securities.

2.d. Losses: Understanding how a loss is recorded is fairly straightforward. A loss doesn't relate directly to the primary activities of the company's product or service, nor is it a part of the daily operations. It is *extraordinary*. This is important as a stock investor because *extraordinary* typically means something isn't predictable. Benjamin Graham would caution his students to pay close attention to extraordinary items and try to assess their impact on a business, to manage and mitigate risk.

A loss is also the result of a difference in the value an asset is listed for on the balance sheet and the proceeds received from the sale of that asset. Let's say, for example, that our soft drinks company purchased a machine that speeds up the process of getting the soft drinks into the can. As a result, we decide to sell the old machine. Since the machine is somewhat out of date and used, we are not able to sell the $1,000 machine for the same price we purchased it for. Instead, we can only sell it for $500. Since this is $500 less than the amount we had the machine listed for on our balance sheet (under the property/plant/equipment line of accounting), we're able to account for a $500 loss on the income statement.

Getting into the details: When the old machine is sold, the cash account (balance sheet) will add $500 for the funds gained from the sale, the property account (balance sheet) will decrease by $1,000 since the machine is no longer owned by the company, and the loss line (income statement) will have -$500 listed for the difference between the purchase price and the sales price.

As mentioned earlier in the *Gains section,* losses are considered non-operating income accounts. Consequently, you will most likely find losses reported near the bottom of the income statement. In combination, the line is usually called *extraordinary income/expense,* as in our example, or sometimes *sale on assets.* As the $275 is a positive number for line 11, we could conclude that there has been more extraordinary income than expenses, or more gains than losses.

So, let's get an overview of this from our income statement that will be affected by the expenses and losses. Please note that the *Net interest income/Expenses* and *extraordinary income/Expenses* lines can be both positive and negative.

Annual (year 2014) Income statement			in millions
1	Revenue	13,279	
2	Cost of revenue	5,348	2a) Expenses from primary activities
1-2 = 3	Gross Margin	7,931	
4	Sales and marketing expenses	1,105	2b) Expenses from secondary activities
5	Research and development expenses	863	2b) Expenses from secondary activities
6	General and administration expenses	538	2b) Expenses from secondary activities
7	Other operating expenses	1,350	2b) Expenses from secondary activities
4+5+6+7 = 8	Operating expenses	3,856	
3-8 = 9	Income from operations	4,075	
10	Net interest income/ (expenses)	(135)	2c) Expenses from financial activities
11	Extraordinary income/ (expenses)	275	2d) Losses
12	Income taxes	1,352	
9+10+11-12 = 13	Net income	2,863	

Looking at the income statement with fresh eyes

Below, I have summarized this information. Don't forget that if you compare my income statement to a random income statement, it may not look identical. Don't let that confuse you. All income statements are built in the same manner, and it is only the names of the different lines and the presentation of the numbers that are different. Most importantly, no matter how you compose your income statement, the intention is always to show how much net income the company has made at the bottom line.

One reason the income statement confuses many people is because it seems that revenue and expenses are arranged arbitrarily. The truth is, income statements are constructed very logically. Let's take a closer look.

1-3: These lines all relate to the revenue and expenses from the company's core activity. In the case of Coca-Cola, this would be the soft drinks sales (1) subtracted by the costs of raw materials like sugar and tin for making the cans (2). That is also why it is referred to as *primary revenue and expenses*. Gross margin (3) is simply a summation of the profit from the primary activities.

4-9: These lines are all secondary expenses. The reason this is referred to as *secondary* is because there are a variety of costs attached to running the business. In the case of Coca-Cola, these would include expenses for doing commercials on TV, expenses for their trucks delivering the soft drinks, and lots of other types of expenses that are not directly related to the production of the product (4-7). Line 8 simply summarizes the expenses (8), while line 9 applies those expenses to the gross margin (9).

10-12: The common denominator for these lines is that they are non-operating. Net interest income (10) can be positive if the company has money in the bank, while it will be an expense if they have borrowed money. That is no different from you and me. As you will recall from the previous section, we sometimes have extraordinary occurrences (11). This could be, for example, a building that is sold for higher or lower than what we bought it for. Since real estate is not part of Coca-Cola's normal business, we account for this as *extraordinary*. Finally, income taxes (12) are not part of the operation, yet they need to be paid.

13: Here it is: Net income, the number everyone is looking at. It tells us how much profit the company has made during the year (13).

Annual (year 2014) Income statement			in millions
1	Revenue	13,279	Primary revenue
2	Cost of revenue	5,348	Primary expense
1-2 = 3	Gross margin	7,931	Summation
4	Sales and marketing expenses	1,105	Secondary expense
5	Research and development expenses	863	Secondary expense
6	General and administration expenses	538	Secondary expense
7	Other operating expenses	1,350	Secondary expense
4+5+6+7 = 8	Operating expenses	3,856	Summation
3-8 = 9	Income from operations	4,075	Summation
10	Net interest income/ (expenses)	(135)	Secondary revenue/ (financial expenses)
11	Extraordinary income/ (expenses)	275	Gains/losses
12	Income taxes	1,352	
9+10+11-12 = 13	Net income	2,863	Summation

The single lines in the income statement

When I was first learning how to invest in stocks, I always wanted a single source that outlined all the terms within the financial statements. Hopefully this next section will provide you with that resource.

As you go through this section, it might help if you pick a company on the stock exchange and print their income statement. If you want to go the extra step, you might even write the corresponding page number from this book next to the accounting line item on your printed statement so you can reference it later on.

Revenue (1)

This line is sometimes referred to as *Sales* or *Turnover*. Revenue is the first line item that appears on the income statement and simply refers to the sales made by the organization; for example, if Coca-Cola sold 10 cans for $1, the revenue of the company would be 10*1 = $10. Revenue is simply the quantity of goods sold multiplied by the price of the product or service. Every time you buy a Coke, you are in fact increasing Coca-Cola's reported revenue.

The above example is a simplification of the accounting calculation, which is obviously more complex. This is because the prices of products and services do not remain constant over the year and therefore sales entries are made on a daily basis in order to record the accurate revenue generated by the organization. From an investor's point of view, this is a very important number. If the organization is unable to generate consistent or growing revenue, it is unlikely to provide sufficient returns to its investors.

Let us now begin an analysis of the revenue. You might have seen one simple figure stated in the income statement reporting the revenue of Coca-Cola. As an informed investor, you might need more information regarding the generation of revenue—especially if the company has a deteriorating revenue stream. If you were interested in understanding why the revenue had increased, you could dig deeper into the 10K or 10Q, where you'll find a section titled *Net Operating Revenues*.

Regardless of the company you are researching, each of the line items throughout the income statement should be explained in the document; for example, Coca-Cola segments its operations according to geographical mix and therefore the revenue that is reported is shown according to the sales that have been generated from a given geographical area. The segmented operations report would help in identifying the segments that are doing relatively better than segments that have lost sales levels.

Cost of revenue (2)

This line has many different names, such as *Cost of Sales, Costs of Goods Sold* (often referred to as COGS) and *Production Costs*. In my opinion, the best expression to use is Cost of Revenue, simply because this is what the line represents. It is the costs that are related to making the company's primary product or service. If you're looking for more details on the derivation of this number, you can dig into the accounting policies in the annual report. It is required by law to disclose how the cost of revenue is derived.

Let's look at an example. A corporation that generates sales is likely to incur direct costs that are associated with these sales; for example, if Coca-Cola sells ten cans, then they must incur some form of manufacturing cost in the production of these items. These costs might include direct raw materials such as sugar, and indirect materials such as tin for producing the cans. Labor would also be required in the production of goods and therefore all the costs incurred in the production of goods must be accounted for. Any company that deals in manufacturing goods would have to make a manufacturing account separately, while a corporation that simply outsources the production is likely to report the total outsourcing cost. The basic concept is that all direct costs associated with the production of goods must be accounted for, and this is shown within the cost of revenue in the income statement.

The emphasis is placed on the term *direct costs*; this is because these are the costs that arise as a result of per unit sales rather than any other cost driver; for example, we can easily ascertain the labor cost per unit or the material required per unit of production. When sales increase, the cost of sales must increase respectively; for example, say that Coca-Cola has direct labor costs of $0.20 and direct material costs of $0.35. This makes the total direct cost of $0.55 per can. If the company sells ten cans, then the total cost of revenue would be 10*$0.55 = $5.5

This example indicates that when sales increase, the *cost* of sales must increase, given that per unit rates remain constant. Be aware that the beverage company will not incur cost of revenue before any revenue occurs. In the example above, there will be no cost of revenue recorded for the 11th bottle before it is sold.

The question that now arises is why is the cost of sales or revenue important to an investor? Well, cost of revenue is typically the largest cost accounted for within the income statement and determines the extent to which the company is able to maintain its direct costs and generate a gross profit. An investor must have knowledge of the composition of the direct costs associated with the organization; for example, let's assume that a company has a very high cost of revenue. If it cost Coke $0.95 to produce a single drink, for instance, the $1.00 sale wouldn't provide a very good margin. If the cost of revenue is almost as high as the revenue, we can quickly assume that the company will struggle to ever produce a decent profit on their product. Remember we haven't even accounted for secondary expenses like marketing and R&D.

Warren Buffett states that an investor must conduct a complete financial analysis of a company before buying stocks. This analysis includes basic cost drivers such as the cost of revenue. Coca-Cola, for example, is mainly dependent on sugar for the manufacturing of beverages. As a result, this means that the company is highly susceptible to changes in sugar prices—volatility could quickly erode or produce profits.

The investor must pay close attention to the trends in the cost of revenue. If sales are constant and the cost of revenue continues to grow, a negative trend is developing. Understanding this trend is the essence of managing risk and return. This will be examined in more detail in the ratio analysis section.

Gross profit (3)

This is sometimes referred to as the company's *Margin* or *Markup*. Gross profit is simply the revenue generated from core products and services less the direct costs associated with the production of goods or delivery of service. Let's continue with our Coca-Cola example. The sales price per bottle is $1 while the direct costs are $0.55; sales less cost of sales is equal to $0.45, which is in fact the gross profit generated by the business. Gross profit in essence is a measure of the organization's efficiency—that is, the ability of the management to control its direct cost of revenue while simultaneously increasing sales.

As an investor, you cannot compare the gross profit between two different industries. This often leads to misleading assumptions and doesn't provide a relative framework to assess a company's performance. As an investor, you must analyze the gross profit, but do not overanalyze the figure without a clear idea of the underlying concept and industry standard.

Sales and marketing expense (4)

This line is sometimes combined with *Administration Expenses* and called *SGA (Selling, General and Administration)*.

While the sales and marketing expense is a secondary expense, and therefore not directly related to the product, the importance of advertisement in generating sales cannot be denied. Let's assume that Coca-Cola introduces a new beverage but does not advertise the product. Consumers such as you and me would remain unaware of the product and Coca-Cola would be unlikely to generate sales from this product.

Advertisement is one of the greatest costs incurred by corporations today. This cost is incorporated within the income statement. Moreover, you need to distribute your product to make it available to customers. This would lead to distribution costs, which would typically also be included in the sales and marketing expense line.

Research and development (5)

Today's world is consumer-led and therefore companies carry out continuous research and development operations. These efforts enable companies to introduce new products and services and exploit different market segments. The need to continuously innovate means that companies incur costs related to research for particular products or services. The development side generally includes the prototype that is made before the actual product goes into production. These costs are secondary costs and are therefore deducted from the gross profit.

The research and development costs incurred by different organizations might vary according to the nature of the product/service for the industry the corporation is operating in. Cell phone companies, for example, must continuously innovate in order to remain competitive, and therefore have high research and development costs.

Conversely, companies that are operating in stable markets would have low research and development costs. Companies such as Coca-Cola do not have extensive research and development costs; this is because they already have a sustainable advantage through a product that has been sold for decades.

Remember the importance of investing in a company that has a durable competitive advantage (discussed in Chapter 4, Principle 3, Rule 2). Doing so will limit your R&D costs and therefore increase the profit margin of the company's core competency.

General and administrative expenses (6)

The *General and Administrative* expense typically has a huge impact on corporations that manage large-scale sales. Let's return to Coca-Cola as an example. The company produces cans and incurs labor costs related to the operation of its machines. This labor cost is directly associated with production and therefore is a part of the cost of revenue.

Now, Coca-Cola has other labor costs too: what about the top-notch white-collar managers involved in running the company? This human resource does not work for free; in fact the cost per person is immensely higher. This salary is not attributed to the cost of production—instead it is attributable to an overhead expense that's rolled into the G&A (General and Administrative).

As an investor, beware of the general and administrative expenses shown in corporate income statements. Corporations are likely to window-dress this figure. Study these expenses in detail and identify any unusual trends in the figures. You might also compare them to other similar companies to ascertain the truth behind the reported figures.

Other operating expenses (7)

The secondary expenses are endless for big corporations as there might be management salaries, depreciation, rent, marketing, advertising costs, costs for research into new products and so on. It is impossible to list all of them separately and still make the income statement a single page.

The *Other Operating Expenses* in an income statement simply refer to all the overhead costs that cannot be categorized into the major lines the company has selected to represent. Think of it as a catchall category for any miscellaneous expense reporting. It could be operating leases and IT, for instance.

Operating expenses (8)

This line is simply a summation of all the secondary expenses. I think that by now you have a good understanding of which expenses are directly related to the product and which are incurred in the running of the business.

A summation of all the secondary expenses gives the investor an overview of how efficiently the company has allocated overhead costs.

Income from operations (9)

This intermediate result is often referred to as earnings before interest and taxes (EBIT). At this point, we have progressed a long way through the income statement. This is an important stopping point because it often gives the investor a great look at how the company can handle its future debt obligations. Since financing expenses haven't been subtracted out of the company's profit yet, compare this line (income from operations) to the next line down in the statement (titled net interest income/expenses) to gain an understanding of the interest obligations (or debt payments). Think of it like this: let's assume you made $30,000 for the year after all your regular expenses were accounted for. Let's also assume you have a large amount of debt that requires hefty interest payments every year. The interest for that debt is $25,000. Based on those figures, you can quickly see that your debt is devouring your ability to save any money over the long haul. In the example of Coca-Cola, you would compare lines 9 and 10. This would show the company's current profit (before the other deductions) at $4075 and only $135 in interest owed to outstanding debts.

This is a very safe and respectable ratio ($135/$4,075 = 3.3%).

So, that was just a short summary of what we have learned so far. Now that you have arrived at *income from operations*, think back and analyze the importance of this figure from a potential investor's point of view. Until now, all the calculations are based on the organization's operations, and as such this figure indicates the profit generated as a result of normal business operations. This is of immense importance to an investor.

Remember that the basis of the organization is to produce goods and services in order to maximize profitability. Profitability will only be maximized when the business is able to control its operating expenses while maximizing its revenue. The operating income is in fact an indicator of efficiency, and the operating margin indicates the business's ability to generate a profit from a given level of sales.

Net interest income/expenses (10)

Sometimes this line is referred to as *Financial Items* or *Other Income/ Expenses*. One reason this line has different names is because you can really put a lot into this category.

In my opinion, the most appropriate name for this line would be *net interest income/expense*, since this line is most influenced by financing impacts. Sometimes this line is broken into two, namely *Net Interest Income* and *Net Income Expense*, but more often than not, income and expenses are simply lumped together into one line showing either a positive or negative number.

Let's take a look at how net interest income occurs. Often, companies have an amount of money that is not put into use. The money is typically put into a bank account or invested in short-term bonds. The proceeds from this are to be reported on the income statement as net interest income.

So how does a net interest expense arise? Interest expense is simply the cost of servicing debt that is incurred by the organization when it takes on debt. So that is the exact opposite effect to the net interest income. More often than not, this line would show a negative number rather than a positive number. The reason for this is that companies use debt as a financing source, while keeping money in the bank to provide flexibility for their daily operations.

As previously discussed in the prior line item, let's take another look at the impact of a high net interest expense. Assuming a company takes out a bank loan for $100,000 and it has been told that the interest rate is 10%, we know that the interest expense is going to be $10,000 per year. If the company's income from operations (line 9) is only $20,000, we quickly see half our profits destroyed because of the loan. Net interest expenses are taken directly out of the pockets of the owners, so be very careful if the company pays too many interest expenses. As an aside, the company would also need to set up a sunk account (on the balance sheet) in order to set aside money each year to pay back the principal on the $100,000. The $10,000 paid annually would only cover the interest on the loan.

Also remember that this line is not only financial items; it is also other revenue and expenses that are not part of the company's daily operations. It could be income generated from other resources like renting out a certain area of property. In this case, the rent income generated from this investment is not revenue derived from primary activities, but rather revenue allocated in this line. It could also relate to multinational companies with widespread operations that are likely to be impacted by foreign exchange risk adjustments in an either positive or negative manner.

Extraordinary income/expenses (11)

The name says it all. *Extraordinary* is something that is not part of the daily operations and cannot be predicted. This may sound a bit vague, but let me give you a few examples. Large companies in particular experience lawsuits from time to time. A loss incurred from a lawsuit is very hard to predict and can be categorized as a one-time event.

Another example would be the costs incurred from restructuring charges. If a company decides to close down a subsidiary, merge two divisions, or for any other reason decides to change the organization, a number of costs are likely to occur. For instance, it could be personnel receiving severance pay. Again, this is something that we cannot expect to happen on a regular basis. This is extraordinary.

It does not have to be an expense, though. Sometimes an extraordinary income can also occur. Imagine that Coca-Cola just bought a new building and land for the price of $5,000,000. A real estate company wants to buy the building and subdivide the land for smaller homes. Coca-Cola is offered $6,000,000 for the land and a profit of $1,000,000 is born. Since subdividing of land is not a part of Coca-Cola's primary activities, it can report the profit as an extraordinary income. When you are trying to determine the true cash flow of a business, many investors exclude extraordinary income in their model. That said, many conservative analysts will include average extraordinary expenses (for example, the average annual expense over a five-year period)

Income taxes (12)

I made a promise. I promised that the income statement was not hard to understand. Don't worry; I am sticking to my promise, because even income taxes are not that hard to understand. Just above the line labeled *Income Taxes,* you will sometimes find a line called *Income Before Tax* or *Pretax Income.* For simplicity, this line is not included in the example within this chapter.

Based on this amount, every company will have to pay income taxes. If the tax rate is 30% and the income before tax is $100, the company would have to pay $30 in tax.

Okay, I kept my promise so far. Well, now it may get harder to follow. If you look at most companies' annual reports, you will probably not find the calculations as simple and consistent as the one given above. Sometimes a company will pay 10% effectively in tax, sometimes 40%, and more often than not, something in between.

The reasons for the deviation in effective tax rates are many. A large corporation located in many different countries has to pay some of the taxes in that country, and tax rates vary between countries. Also, if a company shows a deficit one year, it can carry the loss forward to obtain tax relief. Some sectors, such as banking and energy, are regulated by a different set of tax legislation than other sectors.

So does this mean you should just take the tax rate as given and not worry about it? No. Tax is a huge expense for any company and, just as you would rather invest in a company with an efficient R&D department, you would also rather invest in a company with a lower tax rate. You should look for the effective tax rate *over time*, and not a single snapshot in time. Like most things in accounting, the important thing is understanding a company's tax trends. Look for consistencies—and when you don't find them, understand why.

Net income (13)

This is sometimes referred to as the *Profit for the Year* or *Net Income from Continued Operations*.

You can now take a sigh of relief. You are at the very bottom at the statement. You are home free!

When you think about it, it was not that hard, was it? You took all the different types of revenues and gains, and then subtracted all the different types of expenses and losses. And what did you get? You ended up with the net income. Always remember that income statements really *are* that simple.

A final review of the income statement

At this point, you should have a much deeper understanding of the income statement. But let's just look at it one final time. It doesn't look as intimidating anymore, does it?

Annual (year 2014) Income statement			in millions
1	Revenue	13,279	Primary revenue
2	Cost of revenue	5,348	Primary expense
1-2 = 3	Gross margin	7,931	Summation
4	Sales and marketing expenses	1,105	Secondary expense
5	Research and development expenses	863	Secondary expense
6	General and administration expenses	538	Secondary expense
7	Other operating expenses	1,350	Secondary expense
4+5+6+7 = 8	Operating expenses	3,856	Summation
3-8 = 9	Income from operations	4,075	Summation
10	Net interest income/ (expenses)	(135)	Secondary revenue or (financial expenses)
11	Extraordinary income/ (expenses)	275	Gains or (losses)
12	Income taxes	1,352	
9+10+11-12 = 13	Net income	2,863	Summation

My goal is to demystify the income statement completely for you. Perhaps you feel that there is some information you are missing. Where is depreciation, for instance? What about the income before tax? You will surely find a lot of different accounting terms in the income statement for any given company that is not presented in the example above.

To illustrate my point, let's look at depreciation. Where is that in the income statement? Well, first let us remember that depreciation is simply the loss of accounting value for an asset. Imagine a car with a value of $10,000 that is to be depreciated in five years. This means that there would be a yearly expense of $2,000. Clearly, depreciation is a major expense for companies. So where is it?

It is actually already included! The cars used by the salespeople are included in the *Sales and Marketing Expenses*. The cars used by the executives are included in the *General and Administration* expenses. I could choose to show depreciation in a single line. That would have made the income statement more detailed, but it would also be harder to keep the overview. That is always a tradeoff. Just remember: the revenue, expenses, and therefore also the bottom line, are always the same no matter how they are presented.

If you had the luxury of viewing the full income statement of a large company such as Coca-Cola, you would find that it has numerous subordinate rows for each item; for example, the *Revenue* line item might have fifty subordinate lines that encompass that number. Your interest in uncovering all the facts behind the numbers is a direct result of your assumption of risk and capital involved in the company.

Let's look at *income before tax*. You will often find this line in income statements as a summation line just above the *Income Taxes*. The reason you sometimes see this line is because some find it useful to compare companies before tax. If you feel the same way, you should not be discouraged that it is not included in the income statement above. You can simply calculate it yourself.

As you see, a lot of the lines you may read about in other income statements are already presented in the income statement you now know so well. Still, you may see lines and expressions that you are unfamiliar with. If that's the case, a simple Google search should quickly add some light to your understanding. The core fundamentals of how the statement works are the most important aspects to learn.

Ratio analysis for the income statement

So now we are done with the income statement—right? You can now read and understand income statements for most companies with no major problems. It's great, isn't it? All that hard work paying off!

So what is this ratio analysis all about then? Well, the explanation is actually quite simple. As a value investor, you are not only interested in finding a great company; preferably, you would choose the very best company to invest in—and that is really where the ratio analysis comes in. Comparing two different companies, you can look at which company makes the highest gross profit or net income.

The thorough value investor would look into ratios for several years when comparing different companies, and he will look for trends and explanations for the development. He also knows that, for the most accurate analysis, he must compare companies within the same sector.

To illustrate the ratio analysis, I have chosen to introduce you to the main profitability ratios, and I will continue to use Coca-Cola as a generic example. For comparison, I have chosen Coke's competitor, Pepsi.

Annual (year 2014) Income statement		in millions
1	Revenue	13,279
2	Cost of revenue	5,348
1-2 = 3	Gross Margin	7,931
4	Sales and Marketing expenses	1,105
5	Research and development expenses	863
6	General and Administration expenses	538
7	Other operating expenses	1,350
4+5+6+7 = 8	Operating expenses	3,856
3-8 = 9	Income from operations	4,075
10	Net interest income/(expenses)	(135)
11	Extraordinary income/(expenses)	275
12	Income taxes	1,352
9+10+11-12 = 13	Net income	2,863

Gross profit margin ratio

So, let's go back to our generic example of the income statement. The company has revenue of $13,279 and a cost of revenue of $5,348. In total, this would yield a gross profit of $7,931.

Let's calculate the gross profit margin ratio:

Gross Profit Margin Ratio = Gross Profit (line 3) / Revenue (line 1)

$$7,931 / 13,279 = 59.7\%$$

So what does the 59.7% tell us? It tells us that every time Coca-Cola sells soft drinks for $100, it makes $59.7 in gross profit. That is when all the costs directly related to the product are subtracted—for example, sugar, the cost of the tin cans and so on.

This is a very neat measure to have. Not only have we started an analysis for Coca-Cola which tells us how efficient they are at controlling their direct costs; now we also have a starting point for comparing with a competitor.

If you, as a value investor, are starting to take a closer look at Coca-Cola, it would also make sense to take a closer look at Pepsi. This is where ratio analysis shows its strength. Even though there is a significant difference in the size of the companies, the ratio would provide a comparable metric between companies. Let's assume that Pepsi has a gross profit of $805 and revenue of $1,283. Then Pepsi's gross profit margin ratio would be $805/1,283 = 62.7\%$.

In this generic example, Pepsi showed to be even more profitable (relatively speaking) than Coca-Cola, even though the company in absolute numbers had a much lower revenue and gross profit.

Operating margin ratio

It probably comes as no surprise how the operating margin is calculated. Instead of gross profit, we simply insert the operating margin into the formula. Based on our income statement, we will obtain the following result:

Operating Margin Ratio = Income from Operations (line 9) / Revenue (line 1)

$$4,075 / 13,279 = 30.7\%$$

So what does the 30.7% tell us? If the operating margin for Coca-Cola was 30.7%, it would tell us that every time it sells soft drinks for $100, it will make $30.7 in operating profit. That is not only when the cost of revenue such as sugar and tin cans are sold, but also secondary expenses like administration, marketing, distribution and all the other costs related to Coca-Cola's daily business are deducted.

Again, we could take a look at a competitor such as Pepsi and see how they performed. Let's assume that the income from operations is $376 for Pepsi. The operating margin would then be 376/1,283 = 29.3%. Now, this is interesting! In our example, Pepsi had a *higher* gross margin but also a *lower* operating margin ratio. In other words, this analysis shows us that while Pepsi is more efficient in controlling cost directly related to the sale of soft drinks, the company is less efficient when you include the daily costs of running the business. You, as an investor, might find it interesting to investigate why Pepsi's secondary expenses are higher than Coke's.

Net income margin ratio

Now we have arrived at the very bottom of the income statement. We still compare with the revenue, which is our starting point, but now we look at the big picture. The formula looks like this:

Net Income Margin Ratio = Net Income (line 13) / Revenue (line 1)

$$2,863 / 13,279 = 21.6\%$$

What does this number tell us? Assuming that Coca-Cola sells soft drinks for $100, of this amount, $21.6 will be translated into profit. And keep in mind that we are looking at the net profit margin ratio. This is the money that the investors made in profit compared to money the business collected for the sale of every product.

Let's compare with Pepsi again. Assume that Pepsi has a net profit of $158. That way, Pepsi would have a net profit margin ratio of 158/1,283 = 12.3%. This is even more interesting! For the operating margin, Coca-Cola showed a slightly better performance than Pepsi, but for the net income margin, there's a huge difference.

This must simply mean that Pepsi has large non-operating expenses that Coca-Cola doesn't have. Remember lines 10, 11 and 12 in the income statement? Without even looking at Pepsi's income statement, we would know that Pepsi might have high interest expenses (meaning they have more debt), they might have incurred losses from extraordinary expenses, or they had large taxes in comparison to Coca-Cola.

From this generic profitability ratio analysis, we can therefore conclude that Coca-Cola is a more profitable company than Pepsi when all expenses and losses are included.

Now, let's discuss the really important part with any ratio analysis—trends. So when we look at this snapshot in time, a person might try and conclude that Coke is a better company than Pepsi. Although this could be true for the year you assessed, you'll probably have a better indication of the truth by analyzing the ratios from year to year. This trend analysis is the heart of understanding the prospects for future performance; for example, Coke might have better numbers this year, but for the last five years, Pepsi's ratios might be improving while Cokes are becoming worse. If these trends are stable and even predictable, this qualitative improvement to profit margin maybe of value in assessing long-term risk.

Interest coverage ratio:

A final pointer to the ratio analysis of the income statement is the interest coverage ratio (similar to an idea previous discussed in the net interest section). <u>This is a very important ratio for minimizing your risk.</u> We already looked at the debt/equity ratio, which was one of Warren Buffett's four principles. This ratio is similar to the debt/equity ratio, only this is determining the immediate impacts of debt. Think of it like this:

> Interest coverage ratio—"I have $2,000 of spending money at the end of each month, but $1,500 of that goes towards paying the interest on all my loans."

> Debt/Equity ratio—"I have $100,000 of total debt and my net worth is only $50,000."

As you can see, the interest coverage ratio is an important number because it shows the reality of a company's ability to keep its head above water. If a company cannot pay for its interest expenses, it is heading for trouble—fast.

The formula looks like this:

Interest Coverage Ratio = Income from Operations (line 9) / Interest Expense (line 10)

$$4,075 / 135 = 30.2$$

If these were the real numbers for Coca-Cola, it would mean that the company would be able to pay the interest expenses as much as 30.2 times from the operating income. That is very safe! As a rule of thumb, I like to see a stable interest coverage ratio of at least five times the operating income. That also means that if we compared with a competitor like Pepsi, and Pepsi showed to have an interest coverage ratio of 50, it would not make sense to conclude that Pepsi is less risky. Both companies would be categorized as stable and safe companies.

Conclusion:

As we look at the ratio analysis of any given company, the two important ratios that I like to consider are the net-margin ratio and interest coverage ratio.

The net-margin ratio is important because it shows you the company's profit margin; for example, if the company sells $100 in soft drinks, its bottom-line profit might be $20. This would be a ratio of .20. Or 20 cents for every dollar sold. If a company has a low profit margin, it often means they lack the flexibility and agility of a company with a strong margin.

The interest coverage ratio is extremely important because it indicates risk, or lack of risk. Properly identifying risks and mitigating your exposure will protect your principal investment and provide sustainable returns over long holding periods.

Chapter 7
Balance Sheet in Detail

◇◇◇◇◇◇

I first introduced the balance sheet in Chapter 3. Back then I introduced the balance sheet by comparing your personal finances with those of a company. In this chapter, we will dig into the world of accounting and see what each line in the balance sheet is composed of. First, let us recall what the balance sheet was all about.

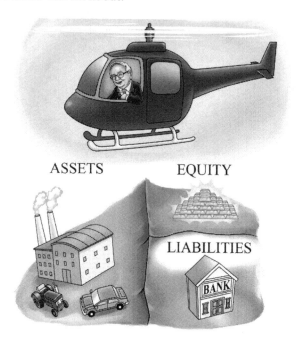

ASSETS   EQUITY

LIABILITIES

Introduction to the balance sheet

The balance sheet is sectionalized into three major categories: the assets, the equity, and the liabilities. In my opinion, the easiest way to explain the relationship is by looking at the assets first. The assets are what the company owns. If we look at a company like Coca-Cola, the company owns a variety of assets. It could be buildings, machines, the cans of Coke that are produced but not yet sold.

Assets can be financed two ways: with the company's money—this is called *equity;* or with someone else's money—this is called *liabilities.* That's the most important thing to understand when first thinking about the balance sheet. Let me give you an example of a simplified balance sheet:

Assets	Equity
$ 10,000	S 2,000
	Liability
	$ 8,000

The balance sheet is very basic, and its mechanics are not harder than the figures you see here. Let us imagine that you bought a car at a price of $10,000. You make a down payment of $2,000, and you borrow the remaining $8,000 from the bank. As you will see here, it is very simple. When you have an asset, it is either financed by your own money (equity) or by someone else's money (liabilities).

Because assets are either financed by equity or liabilities, the two sides will always be equal. They will *balance.*

Now, let's take a more realistic look at a balance sheet. Sure, they might own more assets than just a car, but the principle is the same.

Assets		
1	Cash and cash equivalents	1,847
2	Accounts receivable	3,897
3	Inventory	2,486
4	Other current assets	638
5	Prepaid expenses	285
1+2+3+4+5 = 6	Total current assets	9,153
7	Non-current receivables	1,811
8	Non-current investments	2,768
9	Property, plant, and equipment	8,292
10	Patents, trademarks, and other intangibles	1,827
11	Goodwill	3,235
7+8+9+10+11 = 12	Total non-current assets	17,933
6+12 = 13	Total assets	27,086

Liabilities		
1	Accounts payable	2,183
2	Notes payable	498
3	Accrued expenses	854
4	Taxes payable	427
1+2+3+4 = 5	Total current liabilities	3,962
6	Long term debt	3,211
7	Deferred tax	1,242
8	Provisions	273
6+7+8 = 9	Total non-current liabilities	4,726
5+9 = 10	Total liabilities	8,688
11	Share capital	400
12	Additional paid in capital	3,261
13	Retained earnings	15,590
14	Treasury stocks	-853
11+12+13+14 = 15	Total equity	18,398
10+15 = 16	Total liabilities and equity	27,086

To make this as simple as possible, I have put numbers next to the corresponding accounts. That way you can easily follow how the balance sheet is constructed.

Assets

Let's start digging into assets. When you think about assets, you might see cars and buildings in your mind. But how do we define assets? Well, in accounting, we say that *assets are something that is owned and expected to generate income for the company*. It sounds simple, doesn't it? When I am in doubt as to whether something is an asset or a liability, this is the definition I think of: Can it make money for the company?

That is not all there is to the story, though. Before talking too much about the single types of assets, let us look at the two different categories of assets: the non-current and the current assets.

A current asset can be defined as any asset which is likely to be converted into cash *within a period of one year*. The easiest example of a current asset is cash itself. Other examples include inventory and receivables.

Non-current assets are sometimes referred to as long-term assets. An organization simply includes those assets that have an expected ownership over a period *exceeding one year* and cannot immediately be converted into cash. Examples of non-current assets could be machines for production, buildings and cars.

Why do accountants go through so much effort in order to define different asset types? The idea between distinguishing various kinds of assets is to present to the reader a true and fair view of a company's financial condition. That is also why the balance sheet is sometimes referred to as *the statement of financial position*.

Current assets

Now it is time to look at the current assets. As you will recall, current assets are something that the company expects to turn into cash within the next twelve months. I have chosen to list the current assets in order of liquidity, starting with the most liquid assets first. Once again, I am using Coca-Cola for this generic example.

Cash and cash equivalents (1 - Asset Column)

This line is sometimes referred to as *cash, cash equivalents, and marketable securities*. When we think of cash, it includes both any cash kept in a register and cash that is safely stored away in a bank account.

Cash equivalents are equal to having cash that is currently in a different form; for example, money market funds, saving deposits and deposit certificates. These can be readily converted into cash and are therefore termed as *cash equivalents*.

Accounts receivables (2 - Asset Column)

This line is sometimes called *receivables,* or *net receivables.* Most of a business's sales tend to be carried out on credit as opposed to cash; for example, Coca-Cola could sell soft drinks to Wal-Mart on credit for $1,000.

This payment is in effect an asset for Coca-Cola because it will be turned into cash at a later date. Typically, this would happen within 60-90 days. This also means that receivables, in reality, are an interest-free loan provided by Coca-Cola to Wal-Mart. As the payment will typically happen within twelve months, it is categorized as a *current asset.*

Most often, this line is made up by the credit sales of goods or services, but it can also contain expected current payments such as interest on various securities. In that case, you might see that the name of this account is simply *receivables.* In short, this is money that is expected to flow into the company but is yet to be received.

Inventory (3 - Asset Column)

This line is sometimes referred to as *stock.* Almost all companies have some sort of inventory. Typically, the inventory is subdivided into three categories: *raw materials, work in progress,* and *finished goods.*

For Coca-Cola, sugar is a very important component. The raw sugar that they buy will go directly into the inventory. This subcategory is simply called *raw material.* The value of the raw material is simply the cost of the products.

Clearly, the soft drinks also have to be made. A soft drink is made in different stages ranging from when it is just raw material until it is ready to drink. During that process, extra costs are incurred. Labor costs for managing the machines could be an example. This subcategory for inventory is called *work in progress.*

When the soft drinks are made and just waiting to be sold, this subcategory for inventory is called *finished goods*. Again, additional costs have been incurred to finish the products; an example could be the costs for packaging the products.

When you read the inventory line in the balance sheet, you see a complete summation of all three categories of inventory. If you are interested, the annual report will often provide you with a note that tells you the exact composition.

Other current assets (4 - Asset Column)

Any current assets that do not meet any of the three previous categories fall into this catchall row, *other current assets*. These assets are likely to be converted into cash within twelve months and may include property, plant and equipment available for sale, or any other asset that is expected to be sold within the year.

This category might also include derivatives that are designated as hedging instruments such as foreign currency contracts and commodity contracts. If a company owns derivative contracts, it's likely a way for the company to minimize their risk and exposure to a flexible and unpredictable market—like sugar prices.

Prepaid expenses (5 - Asset Column)

A firm sometimes pays off some of its expenses before it actually incurs them; for example, let's assume that Coca-Cola is engaged in marketing and has paid its customers distribution rights in advance for six months. Assuming Coca-Cola made this payment at the end of November, we would have another five months of funds remaining in this account to demonstrate the distribution that's still going to occur. As this action is consumed each month, this account will gradually decrease and the funds will be realized onto the income statement as an expense.

The prepaid expenses tend to be the most illiquid item in the current assets category. Imagine that Coca-Cola was in a liquidity crisis (meaning they need cash fast). Most likely the contractual terms would not allow Coca-Cola to ask for such a reversal of funds that have already been paid. It would be similar to a person asking for a refund on a magazine subscription that was paid for at the beginning of the year. That's why you'll find prepaid expenses listed at the very bottom of the current assets column; it's the "thickest" and most difficult to turn back into cash.

Total current assets (6 - Asset Column)

Adding up all assets that you expect to turn into cash during the next twelve months for Coca-Cola, you have the total current assets. As you can see in the numbered Balance Sheet, line 6 is found by the summation of lines 1 through 5 in the asset column.

Non-current assets

So let's take a look at the non-current assets. These are the assets that will *not* turn into cash within the next twelve months.

Non-current receivables (7 - Asset Column)

A receivable is an amount of money that the company expects to get back from another party. Since it is non-current, it is money that is expected to be paid back, but not within the next twelve months. Often in business, you sell on credit. For very large companies, contracts can easily be made more than a year, and sometimes the full payment will not be made until the contract is terminated.

Non-current investments (8 - Asset Column)

This line is sometimes referred to as *long-term investments*. Sometimes a company is involved in long-term investments in an attempt to generate income from non-operating assets. That could be Coca-Cola buying companies that are not directly related to soft drinks, for example. Other than shares, a company might have bonds and debt securities that might be available for sale or held to maturity.

As an investor, you are right to question why a company should have long-term investments. You might argue that a company with a high number of investments would tend to concentrate less on core activities. That is typically a bad sign. Conversely, investments such as these might signify a diversification policy so earnings are maintained despite changes in external environments.

Property, plant, and equipment (9 - Asset Column)

This line is sometimes referred to as *PPE*. As the name depicts, it refers to those tangible assets that can be classified under property, plant or equipment. Ranging from buildings to property and from manufacturing equipment to mere office furniture, this is a category of assets that investors find particularly interesting.

A company's non-current assets determine the organization's operating capacity. A company like Coca-Cola that manufactures a certain product is likely to have a large PPE balance—as opposed to an organization that merely resells products or provides services.

While it may seem tempting to own a lot of buildings and equipment, very often some of the largest expenses for a company relate to this category of assets. Tangible assets will often have to be replaced, and that's a very expensive bill that has to be paid. Think of a company like Hilton Resorts. They will constantly have building upgrades and interior remodeling expenses in order to remain competitive in their market. Ultimately, all bills end up being paid by the shareholders of the company. That is why we only want PPE that can produce revenue, not PPE for the sake of owning a lot of assets.

Patents, trademarks and other intangibles (10 - Asset Column)

Companies with strong brand names and efficient research and development departments are likely to carry trademarks and patents. Coca-Cola is a case in point.

The various expenses incurred by Coca-Cola in relation to a new soft drinks recipe would go on the balance sheet in this category. Due to accounting law, a company can list all expenses from research and development as an intangible asset. This means that all the material and labor costs that Coca-Cola incurs in relation to producing the recipe can now be transformed into an asset.

Okay, let's just stop there for a minute. Can it really be true that if Coca-Cola has very inefficient personnel and high salaries, this would ultimately be transformed into a bigger asset? It may sound strange, but that's how it works. This process is called capitalization.

Before you start thinking that accounting is completely corrupt, let me explain this further. As with all other assets, intangibles should always be shown on the balance sheet at the most appropriate value. Capitalization is how intangibles like patents and trademarks are entered into the balance sheet. Just as tangible assets get depreciated, intangible assets also lose value if it is deemed that they cannot generate income. When intangible assets are depreciated, it's called amortization.

This is a very important category and one that Warren Buffett pays particular attention to. Since patents and trademarks provide a durable competitive advantage for a company, it is a great source of risk reduction. Additionally, intangible assets are generally unaffected by inflation. This means that as time marches on, the value of patents and trademarks increase in nominal dollars automatically.

Goodwill (11 - Asset Column)

Goodwill is also an intangible asset. *Intangible* means that it is something we cannot touch. So let's see how goodwill occurs. Say that Coca-Cola decides to acquire a subsidiary (or smaller business) for $200,000 and the book value of the newly acquired company is only $150,000. In this case, $50,000 would be entered under the non-current assets section as *goodwill*.

Then you might ask why Coca-Cola wants to pay more than the book value for a subsidiary. Well, in business there is typically one answer to all business decisions: decisions are made because they are expected to generate more money! So Coca-Cola believes that the newly acquired subsidiary can generate at least the income that has been paid ($200,000) over a certain amount of time. At the end of the day, the value of an asset isn't the book value; it's the money the asset can return to the investor over time.

Goodwill is often mistakenly thought to be internally generated. A typical mistake would be to conclude that the goodwill Coca-Cola has on their balance sheet has been internally decided based on a strong brand. Goodwill only occurs during the acquisition process; it is not something that the company can create by themselves.

Total non-current assets (12 - Asset Column)

Adding up all the assets that are expected to be turned into cash, but not within the next twelve months, you have the total non-current assets. This would be the summation of lines 7-11 in the asset column.

Total assets (13 - Asset Column)

This is the summation of both the current assets (line 6) and non-current assets (line 12). In essence, this represents everything that is expected to be turned into cash at some point in time—either short term or long term.

Liabilities

As said many times already, assets are what the company owns. They can either be financed by the company's own money (equity) or by someone else's money (liability). So here we are again! The balance sheet is perfectly integrated—as a result, you cannot say *assets* without thinking about *liabilities* and *equity*.

So let's take a quick look at the liabilities. After all, doesn't it sound tempting to use other people's money to buy assets?

Like the difference between current assets and non-current assets, liabilities have a similar approach with current and non-current liabilities. The threshold is still twelve months.

An obligation is a current liability that needs to be paid within the next twelve months. Again, I will present the liabilities in the order of liquidity, starting with most liquid first.

Current liabilities

Let us now take a look at the current liabilities. These are the obligations that need to be paid within the next twelve months.

Accounts payable (1—Liability/Equity Column)

This account is sometimes referred to as *payables, net payables* or *trade payables*. Since this account is primarily a category that summarizes what the business has bought on credit, I stick to the name *accounts payable*.

As you may recall, we have an account in the balance sheet called *accounts receivable*. *Accounts payable* is the complete opposite of that. Imagine that Coca-Cola buys sugar for $1,000 from a supplier. If the supplier requires payment within 90 days (NET 90), and Coca-Cola hasn't made a payment yet, then the accounts payable will be $1,000.

In general, you should not mind having accounts payable. "Why?" you might ask. Wouldn't it be better to pay off what we owe right away? I can perfectly see the argument, and most people prefer not to owe money to another party in the future; however, for a company, it is very neat to have an interest-free loan. If Coca-Cola does not have to pay for their sugar in the next ninety days, they can put that money to use somewhere else.

Notes payable (2—Liability/Equity Column)

This line is sometimes referred to as *current borrowing* or *current financial debt*. This line represents how much of the outstanding short-term debts should be paid back to the issuer.

Let's say that Coca-Cola takes on a debt of a $1,000. Over the next ten years, Coca-Cola will pay back $100 of principal to the bank. In this case, $100, which is the payment for the first year, would be shown in this line.

Accrued expenses (3—Liability/Equity Column)

Often, companies will incur expenses that are not yet paid for. For Coca-Cola, this could be expenses for employees' salaries, electricity bills, or basically any payment that is consumed but not yet paid. You can also think of this as the opposite of prepaid expenses.

Any portion of the bill that has not been paid at the balance sheet date would be classified as *accrued expenses.*

Taxes payable (4—Liability/Equity Column)

As an individual person working for a company, you have the "luxury" of the federal and state government automatically withdrawing a portion of your salary to account for taxes. The government might withhold 30% of your pay. At the end of the year, you file your tax return, and tell the government what you actually made for the year. If the government automatically withdrew too much of your salary, you get a tax return. If not, you'll write a check for the difference. In corporate accounting, taxes work the same way, only the *company* is responsible for withholding the taxes it owes—it doesn't happen automatically. As a result, that's what the "Taxes payable" account is for—a holding pattern for the corporate taxes. This is the location where the company will list the money that they owe to the federal, state, or local government for the products or services they sell. Once the payment is made to the government from the cash account, you'll see a deduction in the Taxes Payable account and the tax payment will then be listed on the income statement.

Total current liabilities (5—Liability/Equity Column)

Add up all obligations you expect to pay in cash during the next twelve months and you will have the total current liabilities for Coca-Cola. This would be the summation of lines 1-4 in the liability/equity column.

Non-current liabilities

Sometimes non-current liabilities are referred to as *long-term liabilities*. As you might expect, long-term liabilities are anything the company expects to pay outside the 12-month timeframe.

Long-term debt (6—Liability/Equity Column)

This is very often the most significant line in the non-current liabilities section of the balance sheet. These are simply loans that have been obtained by the company. The simplest way to look at this is to think of it like a bank loan. So imagine that Coca-Cola borrows $1,000 from the bank, with an agreement that Coke will return payment within five years. In this simple example, the long-term debt account would simply be recorded as $1,000 on Coca-Cola's balance sheet.

Debt is a very popular way of financing one's business. When Coca-Cola obtains loans, creditors have no influence on the daily operations. Creditors are foremost interested in getting their money back, preferably with a lot of interest. But the daily business decisions are usually completely up to the management and shareholders.

When you think of long-term debt, you might think that it is money that's owed back. Perhaps surprisingly, long-term debt does not always have to be paid back—and what is even better is that the bank does not mind in most cases! Yes, you heard right. Think of it like owning a home. Say that it costs $300,000 and you have made a down payment of $60,000, borrowing the remainder from the bank. Do you intend to pay $240,000 back to the bank? Well, there is surely good reason to bring some of the debt down, but there is actually no reason to pay back your whole loan— especially if the interest rate is under the inflation rate. As long as you feel that you have sufficient equity in your home, then you should be fine using your money for something else. The bank is usually pleased to be receiving interest payments on your home, as long as you do not default on the payment.

The situation is exactly the same for long-term debt of a company. Let's say that Coca-Cola takes on a little debt at an interest rate of 4%. As long as Coca-Cola can make a better return in the market and can control the risk, they may choose to delay the repayment of the principal to seek larger returns elsewhere. If the company decides to pay off the loan, it would be similar to getting a 4% return (accounting for inflation, it might even be as low as 1%, effectively). An efficient company could probably get a better return by investing in new assets.

That is not the same as saying that debt is always a good thing. It is a thin line, but often even the best-run companies in the world have taken on some debt. The important thing is that it is under control. The metric for determining this coverage has already been discussed with the interest coverage ratio and the debt-to-equity ratio.

Deferred tax (7—Liability/Equity Column)

Deferred tax can be a tricky subject to comprehend if you're not familiar with corporate tax laws. It can be listed as an asset or a liability depending on what year a particular item is being depreciated and what the company has decided to realize as a loss or gain.

Let's provide a basic example to demonstrate how this works. Let's say Coca-Cola bought a car for the price of $10,000. It is to be depreciated over a five-year period, meaning that the accounting expense for the car is $2,000 per year ($10,000/5). Now, tax laws allow you to use a thing called accelerated depreciation in order to represent the actual depreciation more accurately. This may result in a steeper depreciation early on, but a more gradual depreciation later in the item's lifecycle. So, from an accelerated depreciation standpoint, let's say that Coca-Cola can write off 25% of the previous year's value. That means the first year's tax expense would be $2,500 ($10,000*25%), but the second year's would be $1,875 ($7,500 * 25%), and so on.

A deferred tax occurs when there is a difference between the linear and accelerated depreciation approach. Looking at the figure below, you can see the accounting value on the first row (linear depreciation) and the tax value on the second row (accelerated depreciation). The difference between the two values is on the third row. In order to calculate the deferred tax, you multiply the differences by the corresponding tax bracket the company is in for that particular year. For the example below, I assumed the company was in a 35% tax structure for all the years.

	Purchase	Year 1	Year 2	Year 3
Accounting Value	10,000	8,000	6,000	4,000
Tax Value	10,000	7,500	5,625	4,219
Taxable Difference	-	500	375	(219)
Deferred Tax Liability @ 35%	-	175	131	(77)

So what does all this mean? In essence, the tax liability corrects the amount of taxes a company should or shouldn't have paid. When you look at year 1, the company should have depreciated the vehicle by $2,000 according to its accounting book value. Instead the company depreciated the car by $2,500. As a result, the company has reduced its earnings for that year by $500 more than it should have. This means they will pay less tax than they should have. How much less? Well, based on the company's tax bracket, they should have paid $175 more. Now, let's look at year 3. When we look at this year, you'll notice that at this point, the company has actually overpaid their cumulative taxes by $77. It is very important to realize that the deferred tax is only applicable for the year of consideration. Therefore, if the car were sold in the third year, the company would have a deferred tax asset of $77—the tax liability during year 1 and year 2 is already factored into the $77 figure. This $77 deferred tax asset would reduce the company's taxable income, if the vehicle were sold during that year's income statement. Once this asset is realized onto the income statement, the amount listed on the balance sheet (the $77) will disappear.

Provisions (8—Liability/Equity Column)

In a perfect world, everyone would always pay what they owe. Unfortunately, this is not always the case. Companies know this, so when a company sells on credit, they expect some of their customers to default from time to time.

For this reason, companies have a *provisions account* where they continually put money aside to absorb these potential losses. Coca-Cola makes a lot of deals with different retailers. Say that Coca-Cola estimates that 2% of these customers will default on payments. That means that every time Coca-Cola sells $100 worth of product, they would expect retailers to default on $2 of those sales. For this reason, they may put $2 into a separate account—called provisions.

That is not the same as saying that customers will always default. It is merely an estimate for the long run. If Coca-Cola has revenue one year of $100 and no customers default, well, that's great for Coca-Cola—they would still have $2 set aside for when times are bad. The next year, a customer who accounted for $4 revenue defaults. No problem! Since Coca-Cola has set $2 aside for the first year, and also set aside $2 for the following year, this will not affect the income statement. It has already been accounted for.

You may well feel that provisions are not always perfectly matched. You are correct. That is why you will often see that the provisions account fluctuates from year to year. If it turns out that the average estimate of, say, 2% is too much or too little, companies simply adjust continually.

Total non-current liabilities (9—Liability/Equity Column)

Adding up all the obligations that have to be paid in cash, but not within the next twelve months, gives you Coca-Cola's non-current liabilities.

Total liabilities (10—Liability/Equity Column)

As you might expect, this number is very straightforward. It's the summation of lines 5 and 9 on the liability/equity column, which combines current liabilities and non-current liabilities.

Equity

Assets, as you will remember, are either financed by our own money (equity) or by someone else's money (liabilities). As such, you could say that the company does not own anything. When you own a share, you own a part of a real company. That is why you find equity grouped together with liabilities. Equity is a form of liability. It is what the company owes to the owners of the company. So, just to make things clear: Coca-Cola does not own anything—it is the shareholders of Coca-Cola who own all the company's assets.

With this in mind, let's begin to dig into each line of equity.

Share capital (11—Liability/Equity Column):

This line is often referred to as *capital stock, common stock, or paid-in capital*. This is a section that often confuses many investors. The share capital is simply used to keep track of common stock splits and common shares outstanding. When a company is originally started, the founder(s) place a certain amount of money into an equity account called *paid-in capital*. The owners use that money as a representation of the shares outstanding. For example, if the company wanted to issue 100 common shares of the company, they might put $100 dollars into this account and say each common share has a par value of $1.00. The interesting point about this action is that it doesn't matter what amount the company wants to use as the starting point. If the company wanted to put $1.00 into the Share Capital account and still issue 100 common shares, they could do that too. In that case, the par value on each share would be one cent. Regardless of the initial designation of how much one share's par value is, the share capital account is a tracking tool for future splits and share growth/contraction.

To demonstrate my point, let's say this new company has $100 in their share capital account. If they have 100 shares issued, each common share has a par value of $1.00. Let's also assume this company has had a lot of success through the years. As a result, the company's stock price, or market price, has skyrocketed to $500 a share. Remember, this is the market price, not the par value. Although the market price has gone up, the par value of the common stock remains unchanged. As the company continues to grow, they are looking to raise additional funding for future acquisitions. In order to raise this money, the company decides to issue 100 more shares outstanding. Before the company can issue the new shares, they need to check the corporate charter to determine the allowable number of shares outstanding; for example, the charter might show that the company has a limit of issuing 500 common shares outstanding.

Many balance sheets show this number in the share capital line of accounting. It might say," 500 shares authorized, 100 shares issued." Now that we know the company's charter supports the new issue of common stock, the company can issue more shares.

In order to do this, the company would need to put an additional $100 into the Share Capital account to issue 100 more common shares (remember, the par value is $1.00). Now, the shares might sell on the open market for $500, therefore raising money for the company, but that doesn't preclude the company from tracking the new number of shares in the capital account. At the end of this action, there would be $200 in the capital account and 200 shares would be outstanding.

Now for the twist. Let's say the company wanted to conduct a stock split. In this case, the company would double their shares outstanding again; for example, the company would issue another 200 shares—one share to each existing shareholder. During a stock split, the company's intention is to reduce the market price of each share. During a stock split, the company isn't wanting to raise additional funding; instead they are trying to lower the current market price of each share so more people can trade the stock. To conduct the stock split, the company simply issues an additional share to each outstanding share on the market. Since the distribution is equal across all owners (relative to the number of shares they own), the impact to the value of each owner is unchanged. With respect to the capital stock account, only a small change is made. The line would now say, "500 shares authorized, 400 shares issued." The capital account would remain at $200, but the par value per share would now be $0.50. (400 shares/$200 = $0.50).

As you can see, the par value of common stock is nothing more than a tracking tool. It allows owners the ability to determine stock splits and/or repurchases. Most capital accounts use a penny or less to represent each outstanding share.

Additional paid-in capital (12—Liability/Equity Column):

Contrary to the share capital, additional paid-in capital typically has a much higher value when you look at the balance sheet. The reason for this is simple. Imagine again that Coca-Cola has 100 shares with a par value of $1 each. Let's assume they want to raise more money by offering more shares onto the open market. Let's also assume that the company can sell each share for $50 on the market. If the company sustains a par value of $1 for each additional share issued, the paid-in capital account would have $4,900 in it ($50*100 - $1*100 = $4,900). As you can derive from the calculation, additional paid-in capital is therefore the difference between the proceeds for the issue of the stock subtracted by the par value.

You might wonder why investors pay such a high price over the share's par value. That is a completely legitimate question to ask. The answer is very simple: the actual share price of Coca-Cola has nothing to do with the par value. Par value on common stock is merely used for bookkeeping purposes (as previously mentioned). If you value a stock to be worth $50, you should not care the least bit about the par value.

Retained earnings (13—Liability/Equity Column):

The retained earnings are the sum of all the previous net incomes the company has produced. Let me give you an example.

Say that Coca-Cola has made a profit of $100 for the first year of business. If no dividend payments were made, then $100 would go from the net income (on the income statement) to the retained earnings (on the balance sheet). Now imagine that Coca-Cola makes a profit of $150 the next year.

Well, again, given that there are no dividend payments, you would now have a retained earnings account in the business of $250 ($100+$150). We have now experienced an increase in Coca-Cola's equity. Does that mean that Coca-Cola now owns $250 more? Nonsense! Coca-Cola's shareholders now own $250 more, and, as you will recall, equity is simply just the liability the company owes the owners.

So far, we have not considered dividend payments. But say that Coca-Cola decided to pay out $25 in dividends to the owners after year two. Now the retained earnings account would be $225 ($100+$150-$25). That also means that when you look at the retained earnings line, you should not only look at how much the line is growing; you should also consider how much of a dividend is being paid out to the owners. Paying a dividend is simply one method to return money to the shareholders.

Does this also mean that all the money at the retained earnings can be paid out to the owners? Let's take a look at the balance sheet for our generic example. If this was for Coca-Cola, we could see that there are retained earnings of $15,590 in the company.

However, only cash of $1,847 can be paid out to investors. So where did all the money go that Coca-Cola has made during the years? The majority of that money has been reemployed in the business. If this balance sheet was for Coca-Cola, it could have been employed in the inventory for buying more sugar or in a new building for the headquarters. Basically, these are the assets that you see in the balance sheet.

Capital is reemployed by the company to create even more money in the future. As an investor, you should be pleased to see that capital is being reemployed in new assets (assuming the company has a high return on equity, ROE).

Treasury stock (14—Liability/Equity Column):

If there is one line that puzzles investors, it is the treasury stock. One reason for this is that it is a *contra account*. Basically you just need to think of everything you just learned—and do the opposite! It is not surprising that many investors get confused.

Say that Coca-Cola makes a profit of $100 and decides to buy some of the outstanding shares off the open market. This means that if you were a shareholder in Coca-Cola, and you sold some of your shares, the sale might have been back to the company itself. Why would Coca-Cola buy its own shares? Well, imagine that there are one hundred Coca-Cola shares and the share price is $50. If Coca-Cola made a profit of $100 and spent the entire profit on buying back shares, the company would be able to buy back two shares.

In other words, there were originally one hundred shares outstanding, but now there are only ninety-eight (100-2). If I own one of the remaining 98 shares in Coca-Cola, I would now own a larger part of the company. Before, I owned 1/100 of Coca-Cola, but after the share buy-back I now own 1/98 of the company. I am quite pleased with this because it also means that next year, if the profit is still $100, my part of the earnings would no longer be $1 ($100/100) but $1.02 ($100/98). Let me illustrate this:

Before stock buy back		
	Coca-Cola	You
# Shares	100	1
Ownership		1.00%
Equity	$10,000.00	$100.00

After stock buy back (and net income of $100)		
	Coca-Cola	You
# Shares	98	1
Ownership		1.02%
Equity	$10,000.00	$102.04

The reason it may still be a little confusing is that the share buy-back Coca-Cola makes will be shown as a *negative* number in the equity. So if Coca-Cola makes a profit of $100 for a given year and all the money is spent on share buy-backs, the equity for the whole company remains the same in accounting terms (just like it did in the example above for the entire company—left column).

As an investor, you should keep a close eye on the treasury stock account. The number you see in the treasury stock is the price the company paid to purchase each share. In our generic example, the treasury stock is -$853. This means that Coca-Cola has spent $853 from the profit to buy back its own shares.

It's important to note that the amount listed in the treasury account is based on previous market prices when the repurchase transactions occurred. For example, the company might have bought 10 shares at $10 last month and 5 shares at $20 this month. The treasury account would have -$200 listed, and only 15 shares were repurchased; therefore, the average purchase price per share was $13.33 over the period of the account activity. Treasury stocks are interesting because the management can choose to issue the stocks into the market again if they would like.

As an investor, you should include treasury stock when you evaluate how the company has grown its equity per share (or book value). Again, remember that equity is really the owners' money, so by including the treasury stock you can see how much the company has been able to grow the owners' money. At quick glance, an investor might think that a company has only grown their book value (or equity per share) by a small margin— say 3% annual. This may be very misleading if the treasury account isn't included in that assessment. If a substantial growth in the treasury account had occurred during the period of assessment, it may drastically increase the book value growth—which potentially can be used to measure free cash flow. In the Appendix, I have elaborated more on the treasury stock account and how to prepare for this discrepancy in your stock's valuation.

Total equity (15—Liability/Equity Column)

All that Coca-Cola owes to the company's shareholders is included in the total equity. One way of looking at this line is to realize that this is what would be left to the shareholders if all assets were liquidated and liabilities were paid right now.

Total liabilities and equity (16—Liability/Equity Column)

This line is composed of all that Coca-Cola owes to both the shareholders and the lenders. Total liabilities and equity are always equal to the total assets.

Ratio analysis for the balance sheet

Just as we did a key ratio analysis for the income statement, we will now carry out a ratio analysis based on the balance sheet. Since we also know the income statement, some of the key ratio analysis will be based on both statements.

When performing a key ratio analysis, start by looking at a single year. Once you get the hang of it, you'll definitely want to compare ratios over a five- to ten-year period. Also, you'll want to compare ratios across your company's competitors.

To give you the best possible overview before we begin the key ratio analysis, I have inserted both the income statement and the balance sheet for your reference.

Annual (year 2014) Income statement		in millions
1	Revenue	13,279
2	Cost of revenue	5,348
1-2 = 3	Gross Margin	7,931
4	Sales and Marketing expenses	1,105
5	Research and development expenses	863
6	General and Administration expenses	538
7	Other operating expenses	1,350
4+5+6+7 = 8	Operating expenses	3,856
3-8 = 9	Income from operations	4,075
10	Net interest income/(expenses)	(135)
11	Extraordinary income/(expenses)	275
12	Income taxes	1,352
9+10+11-12 = 13	Net income	2,863

Assets			Liabilities		
1	Cash and cash equivalents	1,847	1	Accounts payable	2,183
2	Accounts receivable	3,897	2	Notes payable	498
3	Inventory	2,486	3	Accrued expenses	854
4	Other current assets	638	4	Taxes payable	427
5	Prepaid expenses	285			
			1+2+3+4 = 5	Total current liabilities	3,962
1+2+3+4+5 = 6	Total current assets	9,153			
			6	Long term debt	3,211
7	Non-current receivables	1,811	7	Deferred tax	1,242
8	Non-current investments	2,768	8	Provisions	273
9	Property, plant, and equipment	8,292			
10	Patents, trademarks, and other intangibles	1,827	6+7+8 = 9	Total non-current liabilities	4,726
11	Goodwill	3,235			
			5+9 = 10	Total liabilities	8,688
7+8+9+10+11 = 12	Total non-current assets	17,933			
			11	Share capital	400
6+12 = 13	Total assets	27,086	12	Additional paid in capital	3,261
			13	Retained earnings	15,590
			14	Treasury stocks	-853
			11+12+13+14 = 15	Total equity	18,398
			10+15 = 16	Total liabilities and equity	27,086

Profitability ratios

Return on equity:

The first—and most important—key ratio we should look at is the return on equity, often abbreviated as ROE. The formula looks like this:

$$\text{Return on Equity} = \text{Net Income} / \text{Equity}$$
$$2{,}863 / 18{,}398 = 15.6\%$$

Net Income is found on the Income Statement (line 13)

Equity is found on the liability column of the Balance Sheet (line 15)

ROE simply tells us how much the company has been able to grow the owners' money during the year. So if the ROE for Coca-Cola is 15.6%, we could conclude that Coca-Cola has made a return of $15.6 for every $100 the company has retained from previous earnings or initial investments.

For this reason, we want this number to be as high as possible. As with all key ratio analyses, it is hard to put a benchmark on a sufficient ROE. With that said, you will often see that good companies have a consistent ROE of above 8%.

ROE is a very important key ratio to look at if you are serious about investing. You can read more about ROE in Chapter 4, Principle 1, Rule 3.

Return on assets:

This ratio is also very often abbreviated as ROA. Sometimes it is also called *return on investment* which is why you sometimes see this key ratio abbreviated as ROI. Nonetheless, the formula is the same and it looks like this:

$$\text{Return on Assets} = \text{Net Income} / \text{Total Assets}$$
$$2{,}863 / 27{,}086 = 10.6\%$$

Net Income is found on the Income Statement (line 6)

Total Assets is found on the asset column of the Balance Sheet (line 13)

Now this ratio isn't that important to calculate if you're buying a company with very little debt. In fact if the company had no debt, the ROA and ROE would be the exact same number. As a result, if you're buying a company with a low debt/equity ratio (like 0.50 or less), you can probably skip this calculation. On the other hand, if you're buying a company with a lot of debt, you'll probably want to use the ROA instead of the ROE. If you're curious as to how it works, here's a simple explanation.

For Coca-Cola, the ROA is 10.6%. This means that all assets, ranging from goodwill to the inventory, have been included. Clearly we want this figure to be as high as possible, since we want to get the highest profit comparison to our assets.

ROA will always be lower than the ROE if the company has debt. The reason is very simple. Your starting point (or numerator in the ratio) is the same net profit, but the difference can be found in the numbers you divide the numerator by.

Your assets are either financed by your money (equity) or someone else's money (liabilities). For ROA, you are dividing by the total assets. Since we know from the balance sheet that assets are the same as equity + liabilities, it should be easy to see why ROA is a lower number. When equity is combined with liabilities in the denominator, the ratio becomes smaller. As you can quickly see, if the company has a large amount of debt, the denominator will become very large and the ROA will be very small.

Personally, I like to see a ROA of above 6%, but most importantly I want to see that my stock picks are doing better than their competitors. This means that I would be more focused on whether Coca-Cola had a higher ROA than Pepsi, rather than solely looking at whether ROA is above 6%.

Liquidity ratios

Current ratio:

Liquidity is important for all businesses. Without liquidity, even the most profitable company will go bankrupt. Let's take a look at the formula:

$$\text{Current Ratio} = \text{Current Assets} / \text{Current Liabilities}$$
$$9,153 / 3,962 = 2.31$$

Current Assets is found on the asset column of the Balance Sheet (line 6)

Current Liabilities is found on the liability column of the Balance Sheet (line 5)

Let me repeat here the difference between current assets and current liabilities. If something is a current asset, it means that it can be expected to be converted into cash within a period of twelve months. Examples would include inventory and accounts receivables.

A current liability, on the other hand, is something that we expect to pay with cash within the next twelve months. If we again turn to the balance sheet figures, examples of this could be taxes payable or accounts payable.

So what this key ratio does is compare the company's expectation for cash inflow (current assets) and cash outflow (current liabilities) during the next twelve months. As investors, our threshold for a current ratio is that it should be above 1.0. We can also say that we want this number to be above 100%. The reason for this is that if we do not get more money in than out within the next twelve months, we will be forced to take on debt or relinquish more equity (a fancy way of saying sell more stock to raise money). For this reason, we prefer to have a current ratio of above 1, or even 1.5 to be safe. As shareholders in Coca-Cola, we would therefore be pleased to see a current ratio of 2.31.

In general, you might say that we want as high a current ratio as possible; however, the current ratio can actually be too high. A current ratio of above 5 may also indicate bad money management, as cash could be put to better use elsewhere.

Warren Buffett himself puts a lot of emphasis on the current ratio. You can read more about the current ratio in Chapter 4, Principle 1, Rule 2.

Acid test ratio:

Some call the *acid test ratio* a conservative approach to the *current ratio*. Others refer to the acid test ratio as the *skeptic liquidity measure*. Nonetheless, the formula for the acid test ratio is this:

Acid Test Ratio = (Current Assets—Inventory) / Current Liabilities
(9,153—2,486) / 3,962 = 1.68

Current Assets is found on the asset column of the Balance Sheet (line 6)

Inventory is found on the asset column of the Balance Sheet (line 3)

Current Liabilities is found on the liability column of the Balance Sheet (line 5)

As you can see from the formula, we are now quite conservative when estimating the future cash inflow, as the inventory is not included in the current assets. Let's perform this calculation for Coca-Cola. To do so, we would look at how much money Coca-Cola was expecting to receive and possess in cash within the next twelve months—BUT we would not include the inventory. This means that we assume that the whole inventory of soft drinks does not exist—that's obviously a large part of the current asset value.

Next, we look at the key ratio and ask, "Assuming that we do not sell anything from our inventory, do we still expect to receive more in than we need to pay out during next twelve months? In this situation, the answer is yes. In this example, Coca-Cola would expect to get as much as 1.68 times more in-flow of cash than what they expect to pay out over the next twelve months.

If you are a very conservative investor, this key ratio is for you. Just as for the current ratio, you want a somewhat high value, and definitely above 1 or even 1.5. I would say that the less you know about the company, the more you should prefer this key ratio over the current ratio.

Efficiency ratios

Inventory turnover ratio

Every company likes to be efficient. And inventory turnover in particular is something that the management puts a lot of focus on. Let's see what all the fuss is about.

$$\text{Inventor Turnover Ratio} = \text{Cost of Revenue} / \text{Inventory}$$
$$5,348 / 2,486 = 2.15$$

Cost of Revenue is found on the Income Statement (line 2)

Inventory is found on the asset column of the Balance Sheet (line 3)

If this calculation was based on Coca-Cola's financial statements, we could conclude that Coca-Cola has been able to turn over their whole inventory 2.15 times during the year. As an investor, would you be satisfied with this? In general we want this number to be as high as possible.

As a shareholder in Coca-Cola, I would prefer to have the inventory empty and filled 4 times instead of 2.15. This would show that Coca-Cola was more efficient in turning the inventory into sales. A can of Coke is probably not the worst product to be stored in inventory—and for similar products with a somewhat long duration, a low inventory turnover can sometimes be accepted. For companies dealing with fresh food, you would get completely different numbers.

In all circumstances, capital in inventory is expensive, and for products with a somewhat high duration, I would like to see an inventory turnover of 4 or above. With that in mind, I would rather take this as a rule of thumb and do more research to understand the industry standard.

> Note: It's very important to remember that this number is compared to an annual income statement. If you were working with a quarterly income statement, you would need to multiply the number by 4 in order to ascertain the prorated annual turnover rate.

Accounts receivable turnover ratio

Another efficiency ratio is the accounts receivables turnover. This is a nice key ratio that the cautious value investor should keep an eye on if the company in mind sells a lot on credit. The formula looks like this:

$$\text{Accounts Receivable Turnover Ratio} = \text{Turnover} / \text{Accounts Receivables}$$
$$13,279/3,897 = 3.41$$

Turnover is actually the revenues of the business found on the Income Statement (line 1)

Accounts receivable is found on the asset column of the Balance Sheet (line 2)

In order to make this number more meaningful, let's convert it into days. To do this calculation, simply take 365 days (if using an annual income statement) and divide by the turnover ratio (3.41). When you conduct that math, you'll get 107 days. This means that once Coca-Cola makes a sale, it typically takes 107 days for them to receive payment from their customer. As you might be thinking, that's a slow payment. Without much experience, any investor can realize that a faster payment is better for the business because it puts cash in the hands of the company. In general, Coca-Cola wants this ratio to be as high as possible. A higher ratio means the company gets their money a lot faster from vendors

Like most extremes, there's a silver lining. Since credit typically allows us to increase sales, one must also consider that if vendors are required to make quick payments, they may lose a portion of their sales. So if I had to give a threshold, I would suggest a ratio between 5-7 would be optimal. Again, this is heavily dependent on the industry of the company.

Accounts payable turnover ratio

This key ratio looks at how a company handles its credit obligations, and it is very relevant if the company often buys on credit. Let's first take a look at the formula:

Accounts Payable Turnover Ratio = Cost of Revenue / Accounts Payable
$$5,348 / 2,183 = 2.45$$

Cost of Revenue is found on the Income Statement (line 2)

Accounts Payable is found on the liability column of the Balance Sheet (line 1)

Again, let's turn this ratio into a metric that we can understand. If we take 365 days (if using an annual income statement) and divide by the turnover ratio (2.45), we get 149 days. This means that on average it takes Coca-Cola 149 days to repay their suppliers (i.e., the sugar supplier). In general, we like the idea of having a high accounts payable turnover ratio. This would mean that Coca-Cola has paid back its suppliers rather quickly, and as a shareholder we like to see that our investment has no problem honoring its debt obligations.

On the other hand, a company can also be too generous. Say that Coca-Cola has a good position to negotiate when buying sugar and they are able to secure a very long line of credit before they have to make the payment to the supplier. This is in reality an interest-free loan to Coca-Cola. As a shareholder, we like that too. Long interest-free loans would also equal high accounts payables, which in turn would lead to a low accounts payable turnover.

A ratio of between two to six is typically a sign of an efficient company that is satisfying bargaining power and at the same time having no problem paying its obligations to suppliers.

Solvency ratios

Debt-to-equity ratio

This key ratio is one of the most quoted when risk is being discussed between investors. Let's take a look at the formula:

$$\text{Debt-to-Equity Ratio} = (\text{Long Term Debt} + \text{Notes Payable}) / \text{Equity}$$
$$(3,211 + 498) / 18,398 = 20.2\%$$

Long-Term Debt is found on the liability column of the Balance Sheet (line 6)

Notes Payable is found on the liability column of the Balance Sheet (line 2)

Equity is found on the liability column of the Balance Sheet (line 15)

If this key ratio rings a bell, it's because Warren Buffett puts a lot of emphasis on this metric—you might remember this ratio from Chapter 4, Principle 1, Rule 1.

As we saw, there is nothing wrong with a little debt. Debt can sometimes make things go a little faster, and that is quite all right. Too much debt, on the other hand, can undermine the very existence of a business. If you had to choose, it would be preferable to have as low a debt-to-equity ratio as possible.

When we are talking about debt, we are usually talking about *interest-bearing debt*. This is debt that we should pay interest on. That is also why this key ratio is composed of long-term debt and notes payable. This is debt that you typically have acquired from the bank. You can think of this as the most expensive debt to obtain. Why?

Let's compare interest-bearing debt to another liability such as accounts payable. Accounts payable are purchases that you have made on a line of credit, which can basically be seen as interest-free loans. Long-term debt and notes payable, on the other hand, include interest expenses that you need to pay on a regular basis.

Looking at the financial statement for Coca-Cola, you could conclude that for every time the shareholders own $100 in equity, they also owe $20.2 in debt that Coca-Cola is paying interest on.

In general, Warren Buffett does not like to have a debt-to-equity ratio of above 0.5.

Liabilities-to-equity ratio

Okay, you might have a hard time finding this ratio in other accounting and investment books. The reason is that it is most often called *debt-to-equity ratio*. But, hey—didn't I just calculate that? Yes, you did, but there are actually two different approaches when looking at a company's solvency. Let's take a look at the formula:

$$\text{Liabilities to Equity Ratio} = \text{Total Liabilities} / \text{Equity}$$
$$8{,}688 / 18{,}398 = 47.2\%$$

Total Liabilities is found on the liability column of the Balance Sheet (line 10)

Equity is found on the liability column of the Balance Sheet (line 15)

If this was an analysis of Coca-Cola's solvency, we would conclude that every time the shareholder has $100 in equity, the company would have to pay out $47.2 at some point in the future. This key ratio includes all liabilities. That means that the money Coca-Cola has borrowed from the bank and is paying interest on is included just as much as the sugar that Coca-Cola has bought on credit from a supplier.

More conservative value investors like to look at this key ratio instead of the debt-to-equity ratio. They do like to distinguish between interest-bearing debt, which is the most expensive, and interest-free liabilities such as accounts payable. As a rule of thumb, the liabilities-to-equity ratio should be below 0.8 to be considered low-risk.

Chapter 8

Cash Flow Statement in Detail

When investors think about financial statements, they usually think of the income statement and the balance sheet. Amateur investors often overlook the cash flow statement even though it is a source of very valuable information. It connects the income statement with the balance sheet, thereby giving the reader a synergized vantage point of the company's financial situation. Looking at a corporate cash flow statement would be similar to being able to look at an individual's checking account each month.

Introduction to the cash flow statement

Let me walk you through a short example. You are looking at Coca-Cola's balance sheet and you discover that the cash balance is increasing. Are you pleased about that? Who knows—the increase in cash may arise because Coca-Cola is making more money. If that is the case, you should be pleased. On the other hand, the cash balance might have increased because Coca-Cola has taken out a loan or issued more shares (which diluted your equity). This is where the cash flow statement helps clarify the picture.

1	Net Income	2,863
2	Depreciation	516
3	Other non-cash items	264
4	Deferred taxes	287
5	Working capital	-832
1+2+3+4+5=6	Cash flow from operating activities	3,098
7	Property, plant, and equipment, net	-1,349
8	Intangible assets, net	-214
9	Businesses, net	86
10	Investments, net	-176
7+8+9+10 = 11	Cash flow from investing activities	-1,653
12	Issuances of common stock	98
13	Purchase of stock for treasury	-326
14	Payment of cash dividends	-682
15	Issuances/payment of debt (net)	-120
12+13+14+15 = 16	Cash flow from financing activities	-1,030
6+11+16 = 17	Change in cash	415
18	Cash and equivalents, start of period	1,432
17+18 = 19	Cash and equivalents, end of period	1,847

As you might have already noticed, the cash flow statement is divided into three major groups.

The first section is the *cash flow from operating activities* (lines 1-6). The cash received under this category is the heart of the company—the cash received from daily operations. "But can't we see this in the income statement," you might say. Let me give you this simple example to think about: Coca-Cola sells soft drinks to Wal-Mart for $1,000. They agree that Wal-Mart has to pay the money for the goods in 90 days. While we would record $1,000 immediately as revenue on the income statement, we would not register any cash flowing into Coca-Cola for ninety days. So, as you see in this simple example, revenue or net income is not the same as cash.

The next section is the *cash flow from investments* (lines 7—11). Coca-Cola has to invest in and replace its soft drinks production machines—among many other things. They must continually invest and replace the trucks that deliver the soft drinks to the customers. All companies must make investments to keep their businesses running. This section is where those investment activities are captured.

Finally, we have a section called *cash from financing activities* (lines 12 - 16). This section reveals many of the secrets as to why the cash balance has changed. Perhaps Coca-Cola has acquired new debt; perhaps dividends have been paid to the shareholders. The serious value investor should dig deep into this section before any investment decisions are made.

As you might have noticed, the cash flow statement starts with the bottom line of the income statement (net income), and ends with the top line of the Balance sheet (Cash and Cash Equivalents). As you can see, the cash flow statement truly bridges the gap between the income statement and balance sheet.

Cash flow from operating activities (lines 1 - 6):

Cash generated from operations reflects the ability of the organization to generate cash from its core business operations. As such, we want the cash flow from operations to be as high as possible.

Our starting point for the cash flow from operating activities is the net income (the bottom line on the income statement). Hey, didn't I just say that cash is something completely different than net income? Yes I did, but the net income is only our starting point. As we move down the cash flow statement, the net income will be adjusted accordingly.

Here's an example. The net income is the money (not the cash), that a company has made during a year or quarter. For simplicity, let's assume that to date all net income actually turned to cash for Coca-Cola and the net income is $1,000 for the year. Then, just before the financial statements are made for the year, a deal takes place with a customer that results in a $100 net income increase. Should the net income now be $1,100? Yes, it should. *But,* let's say the cash from the $100 deal was not to be received until the next fiscal year. In this situation, the cash from operating activities would still be $1,000 as there is no additional cash inflow for the present fiscal year. In this situation, you would see the first line in the cash flow statement listed as $1,100, but a subsequent line in the statement would subtract $100 out to arrive at a cash flow value of $1,000.

In reality, Coca-Cola would have a variety of different transactions that would distort the net income from the actual cash flow from operations. Let's take a closer look.

Net income (1)

So this is our starting point. As you will recall, you can find this number at the very bottom of the income statement. From this point, we need to adjust for all non-cash items. All of the other lines in the operating cash flow section are non-cash items so there will be plenty of adjustments.

Depreciation (2)

Sometimes this line is also called *depreciation and amortization* (amortization is the term used to depreciate an intangible asset). Other times, it is simply grouped into a line called *non-cash items*. As depreciation is often the most significant non-cash item, I have chosen to use this name for the line.

Do you remember depreciation? Let me just give you a quick recap. Assume that Coca-Cola buys a car at a price of $12,000. If the car is going to be depreciated over six years, it would imply that the car will lose a value of $2,000 every year. The process of a tangible asset losing value is what we call depreciation.

So this is the trick: depreciation is a non-cash item, which means that there is no cash spent except the $12,000 the very first year. As such, you should add back the depreciation for the later years. Okay, let's stop for a minute. What did that mean?

Let me illustrate this for you. Below is a shorthand income statement where Coca-Cola has revenue of $10,000 and other expenses for $3,500. As we just saw, the depreciation is $2,000 for each year. Let's also assume that revenue and other expenses are all paid in cash. According to the shorthand income statement, Coca-Cola should receive $4,500 in cash…

Shorthand Income Statement

Revenue	10,000
Other expenses	3,500
Depreciation	2,000
Net income	4,500

Now for the shorthand cash flow statement. Here, we add the $2,000 of depreciation back because it was a non-cash item. We therefore get the following:

Shorthand Cash Flow Statement

Net Income	4,500
Depreciation	2,000
Operating cash flow	6,500

When you think about it, it makes perfect sense. $10,000 was the revenue received in cash and $3,500 was the expenses paid in cash. You should end up with $6,500, right? Yes! Remember, the car was already paid for years ago. When that cash transaction occurred, it would have been represented on a previous cash flow statement.

This is why the depreciation is subtracted on the income statement, but added on the cash flow statement.

This simple example is the roadmap to how cash flow statements are made.

Other non-cash items (3)

Just as depreciation is a non-cash item, we also find more of these on the income statement. Remember the line *net interest income and expenses?* It is in line 10 if you return to the income statement. An example of a non-cash item in this line for a multinational company such as Coca-Cola could be the income or expense from the exchange rate.

It could also be in line 11 for *extraordinary income and losses*. Disposal of an asset might either result in a gain or loss when compared to the net book value shown; for example, if Coca-Cola sold an asset for $10,000 which had an accounting value of $15,000, a loss of $5,000 is incurred.

Does that mean that Coca-Cola had to pay $5,000 to the seller? I hope not! The impact of this transaction on cash flow is simply an inflow of cash of $10,000. Gains and losses are primarily accounting concepts and therefore the loss of $5,000 reported on the income statement is added back to the net income in order to account for the cash transactions. The notion is no different from what you just saw with depreciation.

So what happens to the $10,000 which was the actual cash inflow received from selling the asset? Surely we must record that in some way to indicate that Coca-Cola has received $10,000. That is true, but the $10,000 is an investing cash inflow, which we will look at later, and not a part of the operating cash flow.

At first, this line might have your head spinning for a while. From an investor's point of view, you must not delve into the complexities of accounting standards. Just simply remember that some line items within the income statement do not result in an inflow or outflow of cash and therefore must be added or deducted to our starting point, which is the net income.

Deferred taxes (4)

As you may recall from the balance sheet, deferred taxes occur when there are temporary differences between the accounting value and tax value of assets. Previously, we showed this by depreciation.

The thing about deferred taxes is that it is *deferred*. That means that it is tax that should not be paid in the same fiscal year as when the company reports a profit. Or, said another way: if Coca-Cola's net income is $100 and the tax rate is 35%, the company is not obliged to pay $35. Sometimes it pays more, but more often than not it will pay less. In either case, it has an impact on how much cash is going in and out of the company—and this is why deferred taxes are included in the cash flow statement.

Changes in working capital (5)

I just keep coming up with new accounting terms, don't I? "When will it stop?" you might think. Well, if that is what you are thinking, worry no more: everything there is to know about working capital is something you are already familiar with.

The way to look at working capital is to think about current assets and current liabilities—i.e., the cash inflow and outflow for the next twelve months, found on the balance sheet. Examples include the inventory, accounts payable, accounts receivable—basically all that is needed to run the business's daily operations. To make it easier, we call this *working capital*. Now, the name should make more sense. As seen in the cash flow statement above, the working capital is -$832. That means that $832 less is tied up in the daily operations of the business than the previous year. That is good! Working capital is expensive, so we want to limit it.

Imagine that the inventory balance at Coca-Cola at the end of the first year is $2,190 and the inventory balance at the end of the second year is $2,486 (which is the number we see in our current balance sheet). In this case, Coca-Cola would have tied up 296 more dollars in cash during year two in raw materials, finished goods and so on. That means that the working capital has *increased* by $296.

The accounts receivable for Coca-Cola at the end of year one are $4,625. By the end of year two, this account has decreased to $3,897. That means that Coca-Cola has now sold $728 dollars less on credit. In other words, the working capital has now *decreased* by $728.

Hopefully you see where this is going! We can do the same thing for each and every sub category in the working capital. This also includes the accounts payable, prepaid expenses and accrued expenses. All of these are accounts that we have seen in the balance sheet earlier.

The only question we have to ask is whether or not we have tied up more cash. If we have tied up more cash, we have also increased the working capital, and vice versa. So, if the cash flow statement introduced in this chapter was for Coca-Cola and you read the working capital to be -$832, it may look like this if you were looking behind the numbers:

Inventory	296
Accounts receivable	-728
Accounts payable	-511
Prepaid expenses	65
Accrued expenses	46
Working capital	-832

Cash flow from operating activities (6)

When adding up all the previous lines for the core activities of Coca-Cola's business, you get a very important number. Think about it like this: if you were trying to determine your friend's earning capacity each year, you might want to only look at the money he made from the work he performed. That's what cash flow from operating activities represents.

Here's an example: Let's say your friend made $60,000 from the job he performs daily. Also, let's say your friend sold his house and had a one-time gain of $50,000 during that same year. To make things even more interesting, let's say your friend wanted to purchase a new car and took out a loan for $30,000. Now, the amateur investor might say that your friend made $140,000 in cash for the year. We know better than that. Instead, your friend's cash flow statement would look like this:

Cash flow from operating activities: $60,000
Cash flow from investing activities: $50,000
Cash flow from financing activities: $30,000

As you can see from this example, the only cash flow that represents a stable and predictable earnings capacity is the one obtained from operating activities. The other two increases involve selling an asset (the house) and taking on debt (the car loan). This is extremely important—you need to look at the cash flow from operating activities and ensure it's the primary pump for the company's cash flow. When you look at the five-year trends on the company's cash flow statement, nothing spells trouble faster than a company that continually raises cash outside of the company's operating activities.

Cash generated from investing activities (lines 7 - 11)

In contrast to the operating cash flow, we want the cash flow from investing activities to be negative. Yes, you heard right! We want to pay out cash. Let's look into the explanation for that.

As a shareholder of Coca-Cola, you might like the idea of having as much cash in the company as possible. The investing activities reveal the transactions within capital expenditure such as a newly purchased asset or the disposal of non-current assets. So, on digging into the investing cash flow for Coca-Cola, you might realize that the increase in cash comes from selling their assets. Generating cash from the disposal of assets may look good today when cash is pouring in—but if there are no machines available for producing soft drinks, how will Coca-Cola generate cash tomorrow?

An analysis of cash flow from investing activities reveals the growth strategy pursued by the corporation. Any cash outlay from investing activities has the long-term goal of increasing the company's future cash flow. In following years, the purchase of more assets should produce a larger operating cash flow, which in turn will pay for more investments at a later date.

In the following section, you will see that the lines are labeled *net*. Net simply means that purchases and sales are grouped into the same line. If Coca-Cola buys a new machine for $100 and sells the old one for $60, the net value cash flow is -$40 ($60-$100). Remember, the purchase of a new asset makes this row negative. The sale of an asset makes this row positive.

Property, plant and equipment—net (7)

This line is sometimes referred to as *Capital Expenditures, cap spending,* or simply *CAPEX*. You may remember this line from the balance sheet. *Property, Plant and Equipment* is often the most significant line of the non-current assets, and it is often no different when it comes to the investing cash flow.

An example could be Coca-Cola buying new equipment that speeds up its soft drinks production process. It is an investing activity because the expenditure is undertaken for the purpose of increasing Coca-Cola's operating capacity. The cash expense for the acquisition of non-current assets is not accounted for within the income statement. Rather, a charge for depreciation is made within the income statement and the current value is reported within the balance sheet. This is all conducted in subcategories that you don't see on the typical high-level balance sheet.

However, it is the cash flow statement we are looking at now. That means that the cash outflow takes place within the year in which the fixed asset is acquired. The cash balance decreases by the amount of the purchase and it is deducted from the investing activities.

Most often you will find this line to be negative, which is very logical. Coca-Cola will buy more property, plant, and equipment than they will typically be selling. There are rare occasions when you will find this line to be positive; this means that the company has sold more of its assets than it has invested. In general, you should be very cautious when you see this.

While cash may be nice to have today, companies may find themselves short-handed if the funds aren't used to purchase more valuable assets or service expensive debt.

Intangible assets—net (8)

A corporation might also acquire intangible assets in a given year with the aim of improving its market position; for example, Coca-Cola might patent a new soft drinks recipe. That is often a good thing. Big investments in tangible assets do not always indicate a growing business. For many companies, the growth in tangible and intangible assets goes hand in hand.

As in the above case, you will most likely find this line to be negative too. That is what you should be looking for. Sometimes a corporation will sell intangible assets if the assets fail to increase profitability or if they are no longer considered a part of the organization's core operating activities. Sale of intangible assets such as patents and trademarks would result in an inflow of cash and this would be reported within the investing cash flow as an increase.

Businesses—net (9)

Very few things in this world are black or white, and the purchase and sale of businesses is as gray as it gets. Large companies in particular acquire competitors on a regular basis—simply put, it's a very common method for growing a business.

As an outsider, it is hard to estimate whether or not the acquisition of another business is a good investment. Often this depends on how the new business will be integrated into the group, and very few outsiders have that knowledge.

In general, Warren Buffett believes that companies should stick to their core activities. In the case of Coca-Cola, this means that the company should focus on the beverage industry and not buy businesses in other sectors.

I don't mind finding this line negative since this means that more money has been spent on purchasing new businesses rather than selling. But it is a gray area, for sure. Remember, when Coca-Cola buys others businesses, the money does not come from thin air; it is the owners' money! Growth is nice, but growth can also occur at a high cost/premium. This is why Warren Buffett is very cautious when looking at this line.

Investments—net (10)

Coca-Cola might find it interesting to buy shares and bonds in various companies. It may also be tempting to buy derivatives in different shapes and forms. But always remember that it is the shareholders' money. Coca-Cola does not own anything.

As a shareholder, I like to see that a company has sufficient cash. It is also acceptable if some of the excess cash is temporarily tied up in a few investments—I like the idea that it yields a decent return while it is still a part of the liquidity basis. Where managers typically get into trouble with the purchase of investments is when they cross the threshold of passive ownership and move into a controlling share of the business that they don't understand. For example, Coca-Cola's management has expertise in soft drinks and distribution. If they make investments in companies that are conducting financial services, that's probably outside their realm of expertise. This becomes a problem when the company would gain a controlling share of the financial service business and now be the parent company—responsible for overall management. History has shown countless corporate victims that have overextended their level of expertise and often paid a high premium as well. It's always important to use laser focus when finding a business. I'm not implying it can't be done, but I am suggesting it adds potential risk to the owner.

Cash flow from investing activities (11)

When you add up all the cash flow that Coca-Cola has spent on investing in maintenance and future growth for the company (lines 7—10), you end up with the cash flow from investing activities.

Cash generated from financing activities (lines 12 - 17)

If you are searching for skeletons in the closet, this is where you should start looking. You will often see big inflows and outflows of cash in this section. As you look at the trends of the cash flow statement, you'll definitely want to find the financing activities displaying a negative cash flow. It's as simple as that!

If Coca-Cola decides to issue new stocks, it might bring more cash into the company, but the existing shareholders will have diluted ownership. If Coca-Cola decides to take on more debt, it will surely get more cash into the company, but it is you, as the owner of the company, who will pay the interest expenses in the end. If Coca-Cola decides to pay out dividends to the owners, the company may have less cash, but it is you as the owner who receives the cash payment.

As you can see, cash flows from financing activities are highly important for you as a shareholder. Now, let's have a closer look at the individual lines.

Issuances of stock (12)

In this line of accounting, you can determine if a company has issued more common stock in order to raise capital. This line can sometimes be combined with the next line (13) "Purchase of Stock for Treasury." When that happens, you'll simply see the combined line called "Issuance/ Payments of Common Stock, net." Regardless of the naming convention, the line is very straightforward. When this is a positive number, that means the company has issued more common stock to raise money. If it was a negative number, that would mean the company bought back shares from the open market.

Now, let's talk about the important question—how do we know if this is a good thing or bad thing? Before we can answer that question, we first need to understand the basics of an additional stock issue. For simplicity, I'll have a similar discussion in the next section (13) for stock buy-backs.

A stock issue should be treated the same way as a perpetuity loan (or never-ending loan). Think of it like this: if you owned every share of the business, why would you be willing to give up a piece of that equity? For example, you own 100% equity of a business, but you give away 15% equity to raise money; what kind of return would you need to get on that new capital to make the deal worthwhile?

This is the very difficult question to answer and it's often a company's chief financial officer (CFO) who tries to determine this during future acquisitions and financing. In an effort to keep things simple, I've provided a chart that can be used as a rule of thumb for stock investors. The chart provides a quick tool for investors to determine whether issuance of stock for financing decisions seems to be in the best interest of **current** shareholders. By looking up a company's current P/BV ratio and its current ROE, you can get a general idea of the effective perpetuity interest rate the **original** shareholders are assuming for the issuance of the new stock. It's important to only use this chart if the company has a low debt-to-equity ratio (preferably 0.50 or less).

		Expected ROE					
		4%	6%	8%	10%	12%	14%
P/BV	3.00	-2.61%	-10.43%	-18.26%	-26.09%	-33.91%	-41.74%
	2.67	-0.87%	-7.83%	-14.78%	-21.74%	-28.70%	-35.65%
	2.33	0.87%	-5.22%	-11.30%	-17.39%	-23.48%	-29.57%
	2.00	2.61%	-2.61%	-7.83%	-13.04%	-18.26%	-23.48%
	1.67	4.35%	0.00%	-4.35%	-8.70%	-13.04%	-17.39%
	1.33	6.09%	2.61%	-0.87%	-4.35%	-7.83%	-11.30%
	1.00	7.83%	5.22%	2.61%	0.00%	-2.61%	-5.22%
	0.67	9.57%	7.83%	6.09%	4.35%	2.61%	0.87%
	0.33	11.30%	10.43%	9.57%	8.70%	7.83%	6.96%

As you look at the chart, the negative numbers are a good thing! They actually represent a profit rate. On the other hand, the shaded positive numbers represent the effective perpetuity interest rate the original shareholder would assume for the issuance of more stock.

So, let's say you're the CFO of a company and you need to raise a million dollars for a new building. After looking at all your financing choices, you have a few options: First, you could get the money from the bank at a 7.5% interest rate for ten years. Second, you could issue bonds at an 8.5% interest rate for ten years. Third, you could issue more shares of the company to raise the money; assume your company currently has a P/BV of 1 and a ROE of 6%.

Easy enough? If you picked the last choice, that's fairly sensible. The last choice will likely lead to an effective interest rate of 5.22% for the original shareholders. Now, one caveat: the last choice should be treated as a perpetuity loan, whereas the other choices would only last for ten years. That makes a big difference.

So using this chart isn't an absolute science; instead it's a general tool that's based on some assumptions. For example, the ROE is assuming the future investment will yield at the same rate as the company's past performance.

If you're interested in understanding how the chart was derived or how some of the assumptions were determined, be sure to read Part B in the Annex to discover more.

Purchases of stock for treasury (13)

When you find this line to be negative, it means that the company is buying back its own stocks. Once repurchased, the stock no longer has voting rights or entitlements to receiving dividend payments. It is said to be held in *treasury*.

Remember that the company does not own its equity. The equity belongs to the shareholders, and as such it is just borrowed by the company to generate profit for its owners.

When a company is buying back shares, the existing shareholders will increase their relative ownership in the company. Let me give you a simple example: Coca-Cola has 100 shares outstanding, and management decides to buy back 1 share. If you were the owner of the original shares, you owned 1/100 before the share repurchase, but after the share repurchase, your ownership of the company increases to 1/99.

Now, it is easy to think of this solely as a good thing. You would rather own 1/99 of Coca-Cola than 1/100 right? The key issue is that management bought back the share with the shareholders' existing money. In other words, the management in Coca-Cola increased your ownership with your own money. That is money that could be paid to you as a dividend, or money that the management could employ by investing in a new income-producing asset.

To evaluate management's decision as to whether or not to buy back shares, you should therefore consider: How much am I willing to pay to increase my ownership in the company?

Below I have provided you with a simple chart, serving as a generic example to demonstrate the returns of a company's two options (they can retain earnings or they can buy back shares with earnings). To start, let's assume the company has 100,000 outstanding shares, $100,000 of equity, and a net income of $10,000 that can be used for investment purposes. For chart 1, that $10,000 is going to be retained in the company and reinvested at the corresponding ROE. For chart 2, that $10,000 is going to repurchase shares and the company will continue to operate at the corresponding ROE. Let's see how things look.

Expected EPS Year 2: No Share repurchase

		Expected ROE							
		4%	6%	8%	10%	12%	14%	# Shares	Equity
	3.00	4.40%	6.60%	8.80%	11.00%	13.20%	15.40%	100,000	$110,000
	2.67	4.40%	6.60%	8.80%	11.00%	13.20%	15.40%	100,000	$110,000
	2.33	4.40%	6.60%	8.80%	11.00%	13.20%	15.40%	100,000	$110,000
P/BV	2.00	4.40%	6.60%	8.80%	11.00%	13.20%	15.40%	100,000	$110,000
	1.67	4.40%	6.60%	8.80%	11.00%	13.20%	15.40%	100,000	$110,000
	1.33	4.40%	6.60%	8.80%	11.00%	13.20%	15.40%	100,000	$110,000
	1.00	4.40%	6.60%	8.80%	11.00%	13.20%	15.40%	100,000	$110,000
	0.67	4.40%	6.60%	8.80%	11.00%	13.20%	15.40%	100,000	$110,000
	0.33	4.40%	6.60%	8.80%	11.00%	13.20%	15.40%	100,000	$110,000

Expected EPS year 2: Share repurchase

		Expected ROE							
		4%	6%	8%	10%	12%	14%	# Shares	Equity
	3.00	4.14%	6.21%	8.28%	10.34%	12.41%	14.48%	96,667	$100,000
	2.67	4.16%	6.23%	8.31%	10.39%	12.47%	14.54%	96,255	$100,000
	2.33	4.18%	6.27%	8.36%	10.45%	12.54%	14.63%	95,708	$100,000
P/BV	2.00	4.21%	6.32%	8.42%	10.53%	12.63%	14.74%	95,000	$100,000
	1.67	4.25%	6.38%	8.51%	10.64%	12.76%	14.89%	94,012	$100,000
	1.33	4.33%	6.49%	8.65%	10.81%	12.98%	15.14%	92,481	$100,000
	1.00	4.44%	6.67%	8.89%	11.11%	13.33%	15.56%	90,000	$100,000
	0.67	4.70%	7.05%	9.40%	11.75%	14.11%	16.46%	85,075	$100,000
	0.33	5.74%	8.61%	11.48%	14.35%	17.22%	20.09%	69,697	$100,000

Comparing the charts above, you can see that things became advantageous for the original shareholder when the share buy-backs occurred with a book value below 1.0. An important assumption that must be considered during this generalization is that option 1 assumes the retained earnings are reinvested at the company's previous ROE performance.

The general conclusion is simple. Since the company is using the owners' money to buy back shares, a share repurchase is only more profitable for the shareholder, at a reasonable price. If you are more interested in understanding how investors should evaluate stock repurchases, please make sure to read part C in the Annex.

Payment of cash dividends (14)

Dividend payments are perhaps the most popular method for distributing net income back to the investors. One reason that many investors prefer dividends to share buy-backs is very simple: they get cash in their hands. From management's vantage point, they usually have the opposite opinion. Since a dividend payment sends the money away forever, managers of the business typically prefer a share buy-back. Management also prefers a share buy-back because they don't pay taxes on the disbursement and they retain capital in the company to make future acquisitions or purchases. In the end, retained earnings give management flexibility to make business moves.

Let's assume that Coca-Cola earns a net income of $100. The management decides to pay out $40 to the shareholders. If you are a shareholder and own one share, and there are 100 shares outstanding, you will receive a $0.40 ($40/100) dividend payment.

Let us pause briefly here and look at the dividend payments again. We can derive the following from this example: we have a *dividend payout ratio* of 40% (40/100). So what is happening to the remaining $60? After all, the net income belongs to the shareholders and should also be distributed back. Well, that $60 will be reinvested in the company. That means that Coca-Cola can buy even more machines and equipment to increase the net income next year. In most cases, dividend payments will be distributed each quarter. That means in this example you would get $0.10 every three months, and not $0.40 at the end of one year.

As an investor, it's very important to ensure that the company pays a reasonable dividend; for example, if the company had an EPS of $3.00, and a dividend rate of $3.05, it's obvious the company will have a hard time sustaining that payment. Although you might think that scenario is highly unlikely, you might be surprised what you find on the stock exchange. Regardless of the likelihood, if a company's payout ratio (dividend rate / EPS) is higher than 50%-60%, the company might be inhibiting their ability over the long haul to pay owners and still meet the demands of the company's competition. Like most things, dividends are great for investors, but too much of one thing often leads to extreme results and instability.

Issuances/payment of debt—net (15)

As we have seen, there are various methods for a company to raise capital. The best way is to make enough profit so the company doesn't need to borrow any money. Another method is to issue shares, but the downside is that it often dilutes the value to the existing shareholders. Now, let us take a look at the last option.

One tempting way for Coca-Cola to attract capital is simply to borrow the money. So is that a problem? While a little debt shouldn't be a problem, it can easily start to be. Compare this to your personal finances: if you borrow money each month to make ends meet, that situation is bound to go wrong at some point in time.

I would suggest that if you see a company's debt increasing, you immediately dig into the financial statements and understand the root cause. I would take a look at the debt-equity ratio, and if that's now exceeding 0.5, you'll probably want to understand how the company got there and what it's doing to reduce its position.

Another important consideration is the interest coverage ratio that was discussed at the end of chapter 6.

Obviously there are instances where a company gets great expansion opportunities. But more often than not, a steep increase in debt should raise caution flags. This is not the cash inflow you want to see.

In short, if this line is negative, that means the company is paying off its debts. If the number is positive, it means the company has taken on new debt (or issued bonds). This is important: if you notice that a company's operating cash flow is negative (line 6) and this issuance/payment of debt (line 15) is positive, you're looking at a company that's in serious trouble. This means the company's product isn't making a profit and management is borrowing money to stay afloat. Stay far away from companies that demonstrate this situation.

Cash flow from financing activities (16)

Like the previous summary rows, line 16 simply adds all the financing activities together so you can see the big picture.

Arriving at the net change in cash

Now that you understand how cash flows through a business. Let's take another look at the cash flow statement and see if it looks different.

1	Net Income	2,863
2	Depreciation	516
3	Other non-cash items	264
4	Deferred taxes	287
5	Working capital	-832
1+2+3+4+5=6	Cash flow from operating activities	3,098
7	Property, plant, and equipment, net	-1,349
8	Intangible assets, net	-214
9	Businesses, net	86
10	Investments, net	-176
7+8+9+10 = 11	Cash flow from investing activities	-1,653
12	Issuances of common stock	98
13	Purchase of stock for treasury	-326
14	Payment of cash dividends	-682
15	Issuances/payment of debt (net)	-120
12+13+14+15 = 16	Cash flow from financing activities	-1,030
6+11+16 = 17	Change in cash	415
18	Cash and equivalents, start of period	1,432
17+18 = 19	Cash and equivalents, end of period	1,847

To calculate the cash flow from operating activities, we started with the net income (1). This was our starting point because it tells us how much income Coca-Cola has made during the year. We also saw that this was just an account measure, and not a cash measure. For this reason, we made adjustments for the non-cash items (2-5). After the adjustments, we find the cash flow from operating activities (6), which is the cash Coca-Cola has made from its business activities.

To find the cash flow from investing activities, we look at the money that was used for sustainment or growth in Coca-Cola. We had cash transactions for investments into tangible assets (7), as well as in intangible assets (8). Also, we included the investment transactions that could be either additions or new areas of daily business (9-10). Summarizing these, we find how much cash is required to maintain and grow Coca-Cola (11)

For the cash flow from financing activities, we first looked at the cash inflows and outflows from the issuance of stock (12), as well as the opposite effect, which was the purchase of stock into the treasury (13). Next, we looked at the cash dividend payments which were made to the shareholders (14). Finally, we looked at whether the company had obtained debt, or paid back debt to their creditors (15). Summarizing these lines, we end up with all the cash flows related to the financing activities (16).

By adding up the cash from operations, investing, and financing cash flows, the difference was $415 in positive cash flow (17). These are all the cash transactions that took place for Coca-Cola during the year. Line 17 is then added to the cash balance from the start of the year (18), and we end up with the cash balance for the end of the year (19). If you compare line 19 from the cash flow statement with line 1 of the balance sheet (*cash and cash equivalents)*, you'll see that both numbers are exactly the same -$1847. As you can see, the cash flow statement truly bridges the gap between the income statement's bottom line and the balance sheet's top line.

Key ratio analysis for the cash flow statement

So far we have looked at key ratio analysis for both the income statement and balance sheet. Now it is time to dig into key figures and ratios for the cash flow statement.

Free cash flow:

This is an extremely important number! You will often see this referred to as *FCF*. *Free Cash Flow* is actually not so much a ratio, but it is a very important calculation for carrying out further analysis. Many value investors believe this figure holds the key to determining the intrinsic value of a business. Let me show you the formula first:

Free Cash Flow = Operating cash flow + Property, Plant, and Equipment, net

$$3,098 + (-1,349) = 1,749$$

Operating cash flow is found on line 6 of the cash flow statement

Property, Plant, and Equipment net is found on line 7 of the cash flow statement

We previously saw in our example with Coca-Cola that the operating cash flow was the cash outflow generated from running the business. In general, this is the cash received for all the soft drinks sales. As we look at the net cash effect of property, plant and equipment, which is a part of the investing cash flows, we can conclude this outflow of cash was spent to maintain and develop the business (like buying new machines and equipment). Property, Plant and Equipment is sometimes referred to as capital expenditures, cap spending, or simply CAPEX. Although these terms are used interchangeably by many, there are some differences, which are highlighted in advanced financial texts. If you're truly interested in understanding the detailed differences between true CAPEX and the abbreviated calculation we provide here, you can find numerous resources on the Web that provide various methods and opinions. For simplicity in calculating the FCF figure, we simply recommend using the Property, Plant, and Equipment figure. If you find the CAPEX calculation has more utility, you can simply substitute that number for the Property, Plant, and Equipment variable in the FCF calculation listed above.

As you learned in chapter 4, the free cash flow calculation was the main ingredient for the discount cash flow model. We don't include the financing cash flow in this equation because borrowed cash flows are not funds the business has actually earned. When using the free cash flow to determine the intrinsic value of a company, I strongly recommend you look at the average FCF over a number of years. You will find that the FCF changes quite often through the years, so using a high or low number can drastically impact the value of a business. At a minimum, I would look at the five-year average to try and determine the FCF for the intrinsic value calculation.

In the end, the free cash flow can be paid out to the shareholders as dividends, it can be returned in the form of share buy-backs, and it can be used to pay off the company's debt. Basically, it is cash that is flowing back to the shareholders in one way or the other. Cash is indeed king, and you will seldom be sorry about investing in a company with a high and stable free cash flow.

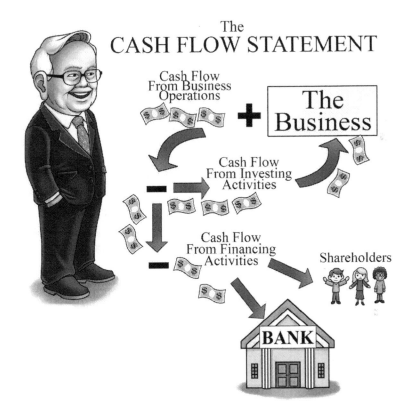

The
CASH FLOW STATEMENT

Cash Flow
From Business
Operations

+

The
Business

Cash Flow
From Investing
Activities

Cash Flow
From Financing
Activities

Shareholders

BANK

Free-cash-flow-to-revenue ratio:

This is often called *Free-Cash-Flow-to-Sales Ratio*. As you will recall, revenue and sales are the same, so let us be consistent and keep using revenue. Let's take a look at the formula:

Free-cash-flow-to-revenue ratio = {Operating Cash Flow + Property, Plant, and Equipment, net} / Revenue

{3,098 + (-1,349)} / 13,279 = 13.2%

What does the 13.2% mean? If this calculation was for Coca-Cola, it would mean that every time Coca-Cola sells soft drinks for $100, $13.2 will be available as cash for the shareholders. This is a very neat key ratio to look at. Not only does it show how much income is generated—after all, income could arise from a sale on credit and Coca-Cola might not see this money if the customer defaults—but this key ratio takes it one step further and measures how much cash will go directly to the owners.

This calculation would show that as much as $13.2 from $100 of sales could be paid directly to the shareholders as a dividend. A 100% payout of the free cash flow will likely never happen because it often prevents the company from investing in future acquisitions or other growth opportunities later on. As a result, the company will likely pay a portion of that free cash flow as a dividend, and the remainder will remain in the company accounts.

In general, you should be looking for companies that have a consistent free-cash-flow-to-revenue ratio of at least 5%.

Investing-cash-flow-to-operating-cash-flow ratio:

Another important ratio in the cash flow statement is found by comparing the investing cash flow with the operating cash flow. Let's take a look at the formula:

$$\text{Investing-cash-flow-to-operating-cash-flow ratio} =$$

$$\text{Investing Cash Flow} / \text{Operating Cash Flow}$$

$$1,653 / 3,098 = 53.3\%$$

What this means is every time Coca-Cola makes $100 in cash from its operations, $53.3 in cash are spent on maintaining and investing in the company's growth. It may be tempting to conclude that this ratio should be as low as possible—or in other words, as much cash as possible should be returned to the shareholders. But keep in mind that investing cash flow is money that is used to keep the business running properly. If no money is reinvested in the company, it will be very hard to make income in the future. Think of it like this: do you like spending the night in a rundown hotel? Of course not—but let that hotel serve as an example of what it's like to deal with a business that doesn't reinvest their operational cash flow back into the business. Companies that fail to reinvest in their business often have short-term life cycles.

How Warren Buffett approaches this key ratio is by looking at the development of the ratio, and at which level it is; for example, say that over a time period of ten years I find that Coca-Cola has a stable investing cash flow to operating cash flow of around 50%. In this case, I would find it much more appealing than Pepsi, which had a similar ratio of 60%. The reason is simple: if all the cash that the company makes is just tied up in new equipment, then I would ultimately not get cash out as an investor.

In the short term, it should not be a problem with high investment ratios—indeed, some years it might be over 100% if the investment possibilities are great. The silver lining really depends on whether there are cash investments for growing the business or cash outlays for maintaining the existing business.

Just remember that, in the long run, Warren Buffett understands the importance of reinvesting capital into the business, but at the same time he firmly believes cash should ultimately be returned to the shareholders in some profitable form!

A Final Note to the Reader

Still got questions? Don't worry about that! www.BuffettsBooks.com is a 100% free online community, with over ten hours of educational videos on value investing. All the videos on the site help teach the same fundamentals you learned throughout this book. The whole purpose of the site is to teach people how to invest like Warren Buffett.

If you already have experience with investing, the forum users would be more than pleased to hear about your advice. If not, still join us. Stig, Preston, and the entire forum would be thrilled to answer any questions you might have.

Appendix

Part A: The Intrinsic Value Calculator and its limitations

In an effort to provide more details about the creation of the BuffettsBooks Intrinsic Value Calculator, this next section is for those who want to understand the mechanics behind the calculation. I would argue that this level of detail will greatly increase your understanding, but is not a necessity for using the model.

How was the BuffettsBooks.com Intrinsic Value Calculator derived?

For anyone who has read Warren Buffett and Benjamin Graham's writing extensively, you'll know they often talk about bonds. In fact, Buffett routinely mentions that bonds and stocks are valued in a similar manner. During the 1997 Berkshire Hathaway shareholders' meeting, Buffett was asked the following question:

"What do you believe to be the most important tools in determining intrinsic value? What rules or standards do you apply when using these tools?"

Buffett: *"If we could see, in looking at any business, what its future cash flows would be for the next 100 years and discount that back at an appropriate interest rate, that would give us a number for intrinsic value. It would be like looking at a bond that had a bunch of coupons on it that were due in a hundred years... Businesses have coupons, too; the only problem is that they're not printed on the instrument and it's up to the investor to try to estimate what those coupons are going to be over time. In high-tech businesses or something like that, we don't have the faintest idea what the coupons are going to be. In the businesses where we think we can understand them reasonably well, we are trying to print the coupons out. If you attempt to assess intrinsic value, it all relates to cash flow. The only reason to put cash into any kind of investment now is that you expect to take cash out—not by selling it to somebody else; that's just a game of who beats who—but by the asset itself..."*

In a *Fortune* article in 1977, Buffett makes the following comments about the bond and stock comparison:

"The main reason, I believe, is that stocks, in economic substance, are really very similar to bonds. I know that this belief will seem eccentric to many investors. For the moment, let's think of those companies not as listed stocks... Let's also assume that the owners of those enterprises had acquired them at book value... And because the return has been so consistent, it seems reasonable to think of it as an 'equity coupon.'"

Although I've only provided a few quotes demonstrating Buffett's opinion that stocks and bonds are valued in a similar manner, digging deeper will only solidify this position. Considering this fact, let's take a closer look at how the market price of a bond is determined.

The value of a high-quality bond is determined by the following variables:

M = The par value or value at maturity
C = The coupon payment
i = Current interest rates or required yield
n = The term or number of payments that will be received

When we apply these variables to a discount cash flow model, we arrive at the following equation for a bond's market price:

$$\text{Bond Price} = C \frac{\left[1 - \left[\frac{1}{(1+i)^n}\right]\right]}{i} + \frac{M}{(1+i)^n}$$

When we look at this big equation, we can see that a simple substitution for the variables mentioned above will provide the answer for the value of a bond. If you go to Course 2, Unit 2, Lesson 4 on the BuffettsBooks.com website, you'll find a calculator that uses this formula. Although the formula is not stated on the page, the mechanics behind the code are this equation.

Now here's the leap: as we look at the comparison between bonds and stocks, we find very similar aspects. Instead of coupons, we have dividends. Instead of par value, we have equity—or book value.

Understanding how coupons and dividends are similar is self-explanatory. But understanding how par value and book value are similar is more difficult to comprehend. Let me provide an eccentric example to illustrate my point.

Imagine for a second that you need to value a bond that has a growing par value. Let's say the bond is issued for $1,000, but when it matures ten years later, the par/face value is worth $2,000. Let's also say that the bond pays no coupon. How would you value such a security if current interest rates where 5%?

The only way we can answer this question is by calculating the asset's future cash flows and discounting these back to today's value at the current interest rate. Since the bond pays no coupons, the only cash flow is the difference between the two par values. Using the formula provided above, substitute the following variables and solve the problem:

M = $2,000
C = 0
i = .05
n = 10

When this substitution is completed, the bond price equals $1227.8. This means that our couponless bond with a variable face value will provide a 5% return if it can be purchased for $1227.8 on the current market. Now, you might be wondering how this corresponds to stocks? Easy. Let's consider a similar question to exemplify:

Imagine now that you have to value a stock that has a growing book value. Let's say the stock's current book value is $1,000 but you expect the book value to be $2,000 ten years from now. Also, you expect the earnings of the business to progress in lockstep with the book value growth of the business. The company pays no dividend, but you would like to receive a 5% return on the potential investment. How much should the stock price be in order to get an expected return of 5%?

Let's do a little substitution for our new problem:

M = FBV = Future book value = $2,000
C = D = Dividend = 0
i = Expected return or discount rate = .05
n = Number of years = 10

When we solve this problem, we get the exact same answer: $1227.8. As you can see, we've simply modified the calculation for a bond's market price, to work for stocks. In the example above, we valued a business with no dividend. If a dividend was provided, the calculation would still be valid. It's very important to remember that this calculation is only valid for stocks if the EPS proportionally grows with the book value during this period.

As you look at the previous example, you might be wondering how we determined the future book value figure. In order to answer that question, we have to start by finding stable companies that have predictable results. This allows us to place a trend line on past performance and use it to estimate future results. If the company has historically grown its book value at 7% a year, then we can use that figure to estimate the future book value figure.

Remember, current earnings and short-term earnings forecasts must be consistent with past earnings performance. If they are not, you can't expect the book value to grow like it did in the past. Your calculations will be inaccurate and misleading. If current and forecasted earnings are consistent with past earnings, they should provide a reasonable expectation of future book value growth; for example, if the company's current book value is $10 a share, and we expect the book value growth rate to be 7% based on historical trends, then we would use the simple time-value-of-money formula to estimate the future book value ten years from now:

FBV = Future book value = ?

PBV = Present book value = $10

g = Expected growth rate of book value = .07 or 7%

n = Number of years into the future = 10

$$FBV = PBV \ (1 + g)^n$$

$$FBV = \$10 \ (1.07)^{10}$$

$$FBV = \$19.67$$

In an effort to simplify our bond market price formula for stocks, we'll rename our variables as follows:

Annual coupon = The average annual dividend expected over the next n years

Therefore C = D

Par value = The expected future book value

Therefore M = FBV = PBV $(1+g)^n$

Now that we have adjusted the variables, let's substitute them into the bond equation to arrive at our intrinsic value formula.

$$\textbf{Intrinsic Value} = \textbf{D}\frac{\left[1-\left[\frac{1}{(1+i)^n}\right]\right]}{i} + \frac{\textbf{PBV}(1+\textbf{g})^n}{(1+i)^n}$$

Where:

D = The expected average annual dividend for the next n years (in $)

PBV = The present book value (in $)

g = The expected growth rate of book value (use .05 if 5%)

n = Number of years into the future you estimate cash flows

i = Discount rate, or minimal acceptable return for investment (use .05 if 5%)

Intrinsic value = The market price you should pay in order to potentially receive a return of "i" over the next "n" years.

Accounting for a steady and growing dividend payment

The formula above is the one used on BuffettsBooks.com for the Intrinsic Value Calculator. Some may argue that the calculation accounts for a growing book value but fails to account for a growing dividend payment. The reason I have neglected this computation is to provide a built-in margin of safety for cash flow expectations. If this is something you disagree with and would like to include in your assessment for value, then this section will provide details on how to perform the math. I would only recommend this method for picks that display extreme stability in all aspects of the company's financial data.

In order to account for a dividend growth rate, one will need to start with historical data in order to establish a trend line. Let's look at Johnson and Johnson (JNJ), for example.

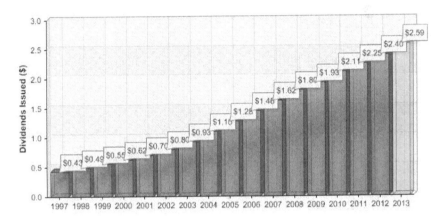

Above is a screen capture from the Johnson and Johnson website. As you can see, this graph represents a very stable and steady dividend history. Finding the dividend history of a company is generally an easy task. I usually find this data on the investor relations section of the company's website. A simple Google search of "dividend history for JNJ" provided a quick and easy link to the above data.

When historical growth looks like this, implementation of this valuation method proves more accurate. In a simple method of implementation, investors can fit a linear trend line to the data then estimate the average dividend for the future term (usually ten years). In order to do this, use the following slope equation:

$$\text{Dividend Growth slope} = \frac{(\text{Dividend}_2 - \text{Dividend}_1)}{(\text{Year}_2 - \text{Year}_1)}$$

This slope will show the dividend growth in dollars (\$)/year

Instead of providing fixed guidance that prescribes measurements over a set number of years, I strongly encourage investors to pick data that represents a conservative and symbolic representation of realistic dividend growth. With Johnson and Johnson, for example, let's analyze the data from 2004 through 2013. Below are the inputs to our slope calculation:

$$\text{Dividend Growth slope} = \frac{(\text{Dividend}_2 - \text{Dividend}_1)}{(\text{Year}_2 - \text{Year}_1)}$$

$$\text{Dividend Growth (slope)} = \frac{(\$2.59 - \$0.93)}{(2013 - 2004)}$$

$$\text{Dividend Growth (slope)} = \$0.184 / \text{year}$$

This means that on a linear average rate, JNJ has increased its dividend by \$0.184 for each year. Knowing this rate, we can now estimate the future dividend JNJ will pay over the next ten years. Since the problem uses a linear growth rate, if we determine the dividend five years from now, we can use this figure as the average for the ten-year cash flow period. In order to calculate this figure, use the following equation:

$$\text{Average future dividend n year period} = \text{Dividend Growth (slope)} \cdot \frac{\text{n year}}{2} + \text{Current Dividend}$$

$$\text{Average future dividend (10 year period)} = \$0.184 / \text{year} \cdot \frac{10 \text{ year}}{2} + \$2.59$$

$$\text{Average future dividend (10 year period)} = \$3.51$$

After solving this problem, you can see we have a higher annual dividend than what the company is currently paying. If we use this dividend in the Intrinsic Value Calculator instead of the current dividend, we may predict a more accurate (and optimistic) result.

Ensure the dividend has a history

One factor you should be careful about when using the Intrinsic Value Calculator is ensuring that the timeframe you are assessing for past growth accounts for a dividend and book value growth; for example, let's assume the book value was growing at 10% a year on average and now the company has just decided to start paying a dividend.

An individual making a quick intrinsic value calculation may assume that the dividend has been paid over an extended period of time. This is not representative, as earlier dividend payments would have limited the past book value growth accordingly. This is going to drastically misrepresent the cash flow of the business, making the investment biased toward a more positive valuation

In order to avoid this dangerous assessment, simply ensure that a dividend history has been paid for the same term that you're assessing book value growth for.

Accounting for growth in treasury stock

At the end of 2011, Carol Loomis wrote an article for *Fortune* titled *Buffett Goes Big in Big Blue*. The article was referencing Berkshire Hathaway's 10.7-billion-dollar stake in IBM. Over the course of the year, Buffett had managed to purchase over 64 million shares at about $167 per share.

As you take a closer look at the financial information on IBM, you'll notice some very peculiar things; for example, the company's EPS at the time of Buffett's purchase was around $13.29. Based on his purchase price, the P/E ratio was approximately 12.57. Not bad, but also not particularly exciting. If you look at the dividend yield, it was 1.7%. Again, nothing too exciting. What about the historical equity growth?

Year	Book Value
2011	$17.31
2010	$18.77
2009	$17.34

What? In fact, if you look at IBM's book value growth from 2003-2011, it went from $16.44 to $17.31.

So you might be asking yourself: *Why on earth would Warren Buffett buy a 10-billion-dollar stake in this company?* The dividend is marginal at best and the book value has barely moved. Since we know from the intrinsic calculator that a solid dividend and growth in book value is what makes an investment profitable, what is going on?

In order to understand this mirage, let's take a closer look at an accounting term called *treasury stock*, which I briefly introduced in the balance sheet as well as in the cash flow statement.

Treasury stock is the name for the shares that the company owns itself; for example, let's say IBM has a total of 1,000 shares outstanding. In an effort to reduce the number of shares outstanding, IBM has the option to buy its own shares on the open market. To demonstrate, let's say the company decides to buy back 100 shares from the 1,000 shares on the open market. In order to take those shares off the market, IBM needs to spend the company's cash on hand in order to buy the shares from other investors.

If the current market price for IBM shares is $155 per share, then IBM would reduce their cash account by $15,500 in order to buy back 100 shares. Once the shares are purchased, the company's equity is reduced by $15,500, and the number of shares outstanding decreases to a total of 900. Now, this is where treasury stock can get a little tricky. Once the shares are repurchased, the company has the option to retire the shares completely, or to keep them in a treasury account and potentially re-enter the market. If the first option is selected by the company, the shares are retired and never issued again. If the shares are held in the treasury account, they will decrease the shares outstanding, have no voting rights, and no dividends will be paid on those shares.

So why might a company want to buy its own shares and place them in a treasury account? Here are a few likely scenarios:

- Current owners gain more control of the company. By minimizing the available shares on the open market, there are fewer shares for new investors to acquire, therefore limiting their potential stake of equity in the company. This tactic might be used by controlling shareholders in order to fend off potential newcomers.
- If the company believes they are undervalued, they can take advantage of their retained earnings to increase the equity of each shareholder. No one understands their strategic position better than themselves.
- This way, the company preserves liquid capital by transferring it into equity. This protects the capital from inflation and automatically reinvests the money at the company's current ROE (worst-case scenario).

So, how should you value a company that's heavily involved in share buy-backs? Using the Intrinsic Value Calculator on BuffettsBooks.com is likely going to have skewed results because the cash flow is not being reflected in the company's book value. In this case, I would simply use the DCF model, which was introduced in Chapter 4, Principle 4, Rule 5. Keep in mind, though, that buy-back programs as heavy as IBM's are very rare.

APPENDIX

Using the calculator for high-growth companies

"It gets very dangerous to assume high growth rates...—that's where people get into a lot of trouble. The idea of projecting extremely high growth rates for a long period of time has cost investors an awful lot of money. Go look at top companies fifty years ago: how many have grown at 10% for a long time? And [those that have grown] 15% is very rarified."

-Warren Buffett

If there is one thing that can severely distort your intrinsic value calculation, it's using a large and unrealistic growth rate. If using this DCF model, this would be your second and fifth input. If using the BuffettsBooks calculator, this would be the input for the average percent change in book value per year. As you can see from Buffett's quote above, many investors get themselves into trouble when assuming a company will have the capacity to earn at an accelerated pace for an extended period of time.

As many people already know, when a company produces an enormous profit and therefore grows at a rapid speed, it has an interesting consequence: competitors take notice. Take Apple, for example: from 2008—2012, Apple experienced explosive earnings growth due to the advent of smart phones and smart tablets. At the time, no other company had a comparable product that could match the quality and performance of an iPhone and iPad. As the market matured, in 4-5 years, Google, Samsung, and Amazon emerged with products that started to eat away at Apple's dominance in the field. When we look at this example, the learning point is this; be very cautious when assigning high growth rates for long periods of time.

In general, the DCF intrinsic value calculator will model a high-growth company better than the BuffettsBooks intrinsic value calculator. For example, if you would like the DCF model to assume a company would have a very high growth rate (25%) for three more years, you could then set a modest long-term growth rate (3%) for all the years beyond that. In the end, remember your ABCs: be *accurate*, be *balanced*, and be *careful*.

Theoretical infinite growth

This is actually a classical problem discussed amongst economists, and is referred to as the *Saint Petersburg paradox*. It simply states that as long as time is infinite, everything else is infinite.

For the intrinsic calculator, this can be translated as meaning that as long as the discount rate is lower than the estimated growth rate, the value of the stock is unlimited if the time horizon is also unlimited. Let me give you an example:

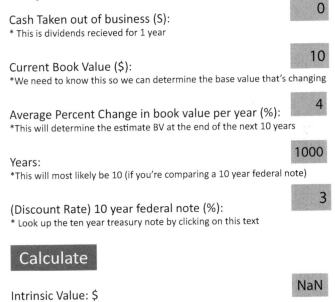

Cash Taken out of business (S):
* This is dividends recieved for 1 year
0

Current Book Value ($):
*We need to know this so we can determine the base value that's changing
10

Average Percent Change in book value per year (%):
*This will determine the estimate BV at the end of the next 10 years
4

Years:
*This will most likely be 10 (if you're comparing a 10 year federal note)
1000

(Discount Rate) 10 year federal note (%):
* Look up the ten year treasury note by clicking on this text
3

Calculate

Intrinsic Value: $
NaN

For simplicity, I have omitted the dividend, but as you can see, even with a marginally higher average change in book value compared to the discount rate, the intrinsic value is approaching infinite as long as you have a sufficiently long-term horizon.

APPENDIX

So what's the takeaway? My opinion is that any model is only as good as the inputs you provide. If you assume a company will grow by 30% every year, clearly you will find a high intrinsic value, even though it is not realistic. If you assume that your time horizon is long enough, you will find as high an intrinsic value as you wish.

APPENDIX

Part B: How to Assess Stock Issuance

In this line of accounting, you can determine whether a company has issued or sold more common stock in order to raise capital. Let's first talk about the issuance of more shares. Although some might not think of this action as a financing activity, they might be surprised. The best way to think of any additional stock offering is to treat it like the company is taking out a loan. The only difference with this type of loan is that the interest rate is for perpetuity—or forever. As we think about the impact that a never-ending-term loan could have on a business, we quickly realize that the most important consideration is the level of interest rate we would need to pay. So how could we figure that out?

Let's make some assumptions: assume the company has $100,000 equity; the equity produces a net income (or profit) of $10,000 a year; and there are 100,000 shares outstanding that trade for 10 times earnings (or a P/E = 10). The company needs to raise more money for a new venture; as a result, they issue 15,000 new shares. Based on the information provided, we know that the earnings per share (EPS) are $0.10. We also know that the shares are trading at $1.00 each (EPS*P/E). As a result, the issuance of 15,000 more shares will generally raise $15,000 more dollars. The exact amount is arguable, because the company may get more or less than that amount as the new shares are traded on the open market.

So, let's estimate the interest rate on that $15,000 loan! Prior to the issuance of more shares, the company was earning $10,000 a year. The number of shares changed from 100,000 to 115,000; therefore the original owners (or shareholders) now only own 86.96% of their previous stake in the company. Based on that reduction of equity, their claim on the $10,000 of earnings is now only $8,696. If (and it's a *huge* if), the company's earnings remain constant, the previous shareholders would be paying $1304 on a $15,000 loan annually. That equates to an 8.7% perpetuity loan—that's ugly. But wait! It might not be that bad...

So here's where an understanding of assumptions is very important. Although the previous shareholders have reduced their share of the company, they've also raised more money to invest into new assets. As a result, let's assume the managers have made a wise decision and purchased a new machine with the new funding and it adds to the previous profit. To play nice, we will assume the new investment matches the previous return on equity of 10%. That means the new $15,000 asset will produce an additional profit of $1,500 annually. Now, as we reassess the terms of our "loan," we get a significantly different result.

If you remember, the original owners of the business earned a profit of $10,000 a year. After the new issue of stock, the original owner's equity decreased to 86.96%. Although the decrease in equity occurred, the company was able to increase its earnings capacity due to the new asset that was purchased. A year later, the whole company's earnings increased to $11,500 a year. As a result, after a year, the previous owners recuperated their original earnings capacity of $10,000 ($11,500 * 86.96% = $10,000).

Now, that was a lot of math. Although that might be a little tricky to do, there's no easy way around determining whether a new stock issue is going to be good or bad for the company. As you can see, many assumptions were made; for example, we assumed the company could quickly (1 year) turn the raised capital ($15,000) into a return that matched previous results (10%)—that's a lot of assumptions. Assuming that didn't happen, you can quickly see how that 8.7% interest rate would have extended into multiple years.

More importantly, this entire situation was dependent on fairly stable factors; for example, let's assume the company only raised $10,000 (instead of $15,000) for the same number of shares; or assume the company could only earn a 5% return with the money raised. All those factors will have a drastic impact on the perpetuity loan. Below is a chart that outlines the differences that would have occurred for the original shareholders of the business as each of the assumptions changed.

Capital Raised from issuance (15K shares)	1st year's interest rate
$25,000	5.22%
$20,000	6.52%
$15,000	8.70%
$10,000	13.04%
$5,000	26.09%

The highlighted line is from the assumptions we used in the example.

The table above accounts for the interest for the first year. Assuming the company can turn the capital into an asset that will produce a return, the table below demonstrates the subsequent years' annual interest rate.

		Return rate on the newly raised capital					
		4%	6%	8%	10%	12%	14%
Capital Raised from issuance (15k shares)	$25,000	4.35%	0.00%	-4.35%	-8.70%	-13.04%	-17.39%
	$20,000	6.09%	2.61%	-0.87%	-4.35%	-7.83%	-11.30%
	$15,000	7.83%	5.22%	2.61%	0.00%	-2.61%	-5.22%
	$10,000	9.57%	7.83%	6.09%	4.35%	2.61%	0.87%
	$5,000	11.30%	10.43%	9.57%	8.70%	7.83%	6.96%

Looking at this table, you can see the highlighted areas represent the figures we used in the example. Be careful—the numbers might be a little counter-intuitive. The negative interest rates in the table represent the perpetuity profit that will be made on the stock issue—*if* the assumptions were different in the example. On the flip side, the positive numbers represent the effective interest rate that the previous owners would be paying based on the issuance—not good.

Although this table works great for the example provided in the book, how can I use this for my ordinary stock picks? Simple: I've adapted these charts so they're applicable to terms and ratios you'll find in a per share basis.

	Expected ROE					
P/BV	4%	6%	8%	10%	12%	14%
3.00	-2.61%	-10.43%	-18.26%	-26.09%	-33.91%	-41.74%
2.67	-0.87%	-7.83%	-14.78%	-21.74%	-28.70%	-35.65%
2.33	0.87%	-5.22%	-11.30%	-17.39%	-23.48%	-29.57%
2.00	2.61%	-2.61%	-7.83%	-13.04%	-18.26%	-23.48%
1.67	4.35%	0.00%	-4.35%	-8.70%	-13.04%	-17.39%
1.33	6.09%	2.61%	-0.87%	-4.35%	-7.83%	-11.30%
1.00	7.83%	5.22%	2.61%	0.00%	-2.61%	-5.22%
0.67	9.57%	7.83%	6.09%	4.35%	2.61%	0.87%
0.33	11.30%	10.43%	9.57%	8.70%	7.83%	6.96%

Part C. How to think about a share repurchase

As with many things in stock investing, there are no absolute metrics that say a share repurchase adds a quantifiable value. As we have already seen in the previous tables from chapter 8, the main criteria are based on the price that the company pays for buying back its own stock.

Expected EPS Year 2: No Share repurchase

P/BV	Expected ROE						# Shares	Equity
	4%	6%	8%	10%	12%	14%		
3.00	4.40%	6.60%	8.80%	11.00%	13.20%	15.40%	100,000	$110,000
2.67	4.40%	6.60%	8.80%	11.00%	13.20%	15.40%	100,000	$110,000
2.33	4.40%	6.60%	8.80%	11.00%	13.20%	15.40%	100,000	$110,000
2.00	4.40%	6.60%	8.80%	11.00%	13.20%	15.40%	100,000	$110,000
1.67	4.40%	6.60%	8.80%	11.00%	13.20%	15.40%	100,000	$110,000
1.33	4.40%	6.60%	8.80%	11.00%	13.20%	15.40%	100,000	$110,000
1.00	4.40%	6.60%	8.80%	11.00%	13.20%	15.40%	100,000	$110,000
0.67	4.40%	6.60%	8.80%	11.00%	13.20%	15.40%	100,000	$110,000
0.33	4.40%	6.60%	8.80%	11.00%	13.20%	15.40%	100,000	$110,000

Expected EPS year 2: Share repurchase

P/BV	Expected ROE						# Shares	Equity
	4%	6%	8%	10%	12%	14%		
3.00	4.14%	6.21%	8.28%	10.34%	12.41%	14.48%	96,667	$100,000
2.67	4.16%	6.23%	8.31%	10.39%	12.47%	14.54%	96,255	$100,000
2.33	4.18%	6.27%	8.36%	10.45%	12.54%	14.63%	95,708	$100,000
2.00	4.21%	6.32%	8.42%	10.53%	12.63%	14.74%	95,000	$100,000
1.67	4.25%	6.38%	8.51%	10.64%	12.76%	14.89%	94,012	$100,000
1.33	4.33%	6.49%	8.65%	10.81%	12.98%	15.14%	92,481	$100,000
1.00	4.44%	6.67%	8.89%	11.11%	13.33%	15.56%	90,000	$100,000
0.67	4.70%	7.05%	9.40%	11.75%	14.11%	16.46%	85,075	$100,000
0.33	5.74%	8.61%	11.48%	14.35%	17.22%	20.09%	69,697	$100,000

The reason price is so important in determining the value of a share buy-back is due to the idea of *opportunity costs*. For example: When you buy a stock, you had the opportunity to buy a bond instead. The yield of that bond is an opportunity cost to you.

When dealing with a share repurchase, you are faced with the opportunity costs of receiving the earnings from your shares as a dividend.

When a company makes a profit, the money can go two places. First, the money can be paid directly to the shareholders. This is called a *dividend*. Typically, a dividend is paid to the shareholders four times a year. The second place the company's profits can go is into the corporate bank account. This is called *retained earnings* on the balance sheet. The intent of a company that retains earnings is to enable it to reinvest the money for you. Keeping the money inside the company enables it to benefit from unique advantages such as tax shelters. If you're interested in knowing how well management is reinvesting the retained earnings, simply look at the ROE.

Receiving dividends is great. Money is deposited into your bank account each quarter, and it gives you a lot of flexibility to move your money around to the best investments. It also has the added bonus of disciplining the management to keep a strict control on their cash and only engage in the most value- enhancing activities. Managers are just like the rest of us. When there is too much money lying around, they sometimes spend it foolishly.

So shouldn't any investor strive for a management that favors dividends as much as possible? Unfortunately, it's not that simple. A huge counterargument for large dividend payments is the tax implications. Every time a dividend is paid, you get double-taxed. The first tax is paid by the corporation (which you own as a shareholder). The second tax is paid when you receive the dividend in your individual bank account.

Now, you might be getting confused as to whether you should favor a dividend or stock repurchase, but don't worry—there are truly good points for both sides of the argument. So, let's get back to where we started in chapter 8 with a share repurchase. As an investor, you want to buy stocks at a *price* below the *value*, and clearly you want management to do the same thing. If that is not possible, you should opt to receive the company's earnings as a dividend in cash, so you have the option to buy another undervalued stock on the market.

APPENDIX

In the annual report, you can find a specification about the dividend and share repurchase policies. For any given year, you can find the money used for both dividend payouts and share repurchases in the cash flow statement.